HMS BELFAST
ON **D-DAY**

This book is dedicated to my father

DM940869 SA(S) Terry 'Taff' Hewitt, HMS *Eagle*, 1955

For inspiring a lifelong fascination with naval history

HMS BELFAST
ON D-DAY

Nick Hewitt

I would like first and foremost to thank the many HMS *Belfast* veterans who so generously shared their experiences with Imperial War Museums over the years, and the dedicated staff from the Sound Archive who interviewed them. Without them this book would never have happened. Thanks also to Ngaire for once again patiently proof reading the first draft, and the legendary Terry Charman for proof reading the final version – I shall always be proud that this was the last IWM title on which Terry worked his magic before retirement! I am hugely grateful to the super-efficient Miranda for her copy-editing, and to all my former IWM colleagues who have helped out, notably Tony Richards for locating some lost treasures in the archives and providing scans in record time. Finally, many thanks to Liz and Caitlin from IWM Publishing, for letting me have this wonderful opportunity to give something back to HMS *Belfast*, where I had the great privilege of working for five fantastic years.

Published by IWM, Lambeth Road, London SE1 6HZ
iwm.org.uk

ISBN 978-1-912423-77-4

A catalogue record for this book is available from the British Library

Colour reproduction by DL Imaging
Printed and bound by Printer Trento, Italy

All images © IWM unless otherwise stated
Front cover illustration: Matt Carr
Back cover image: A 23916 (colourised)

CONTENTS

INTRODUCTION

Operation 'Overlord' – the code name given to the Allied liberation of German-occupied north-west Europe on 6 June 1944 – was arguably the most challenging, complicated and risky military operation in history. It has of course gone down in history as 'D-Day', although there have been and continue to be many 'D-Days', the term simply being military shorthand for the first day of any major operation. But for most of us, there is only one.

The scale of 'Overlord' was staggering. The operation involved safely landing 156,000 troops on 50 miles of coastline, fortified and strongly defended by an enemy which had been preparing for this day for years. 20,000 of these soldiers were paratroops but the vast majority landed from, and were supported or sustained by, a gigantic fleet of nearly 7,000 warships, merchant ships and specialised amphibious assault vessels. By the end of 11 June, this armada had put ashore a staggering 326,547 troops, 54,186 vehicles and 104,428 tons of supplies, more than were deployed to liberate Kuwait in 1991 or invade Iraq in 2003.

D-Day is a key twentieth-century story, but one for which the popular cultural references have been drawn almost overwhelmingly from the land battle, influenced heavily, perhaps, by films such as *Saving Private Ryan* and *The Longest Day*. In short, D-Day is usually coloured 'army green', despite the fact that responsibility for transporting that army, getting it safely ashore, providing the kind of overwhelming firepower which allowed a small amphibious force to win major engagements against a better armed and more numerous foe, and keeping them supplied and equipped to fight for months without a friendly port, rested with the naval forces. This naval element of 'Overlord' was codenamed Operation 'Neptune'.

While the US Navy took the lead in the sweeping, complex operations against the Japanese in the Pacific, much of the naval effort in the European war was made by the Royal Navy, supported by smaller US and Allied forces. 79 per cent of the naval power which facilitated Operation 'Neptune' was British or Canadian, including 892 out of 1,213 major warships, and 3,261 out of 4,126 landing craft.

To paraphrase the commander-in-chief of an earlier and failed amphibious operation (Sir Ian Hamilton's First Gallipoli Despatch, 20 May 1915), the Royal Navy was 'father and mother to the Army [and] risked everything to give their soldier comrades a fair run in at the enemy'.

Of these thousands of naval and merchant ships, less than 25 are thought to exist today (see Appendix 1 for a full list of known D-Day survivors). Of these, the most significant Royal Navy survivor is the cruiser HMS *Belfast*, now moored in the Pool of London as a branch of IWM. While *Belfast* could be thought of as a 'silent witness', her former crew are most certainly not, and over the years the IWM Sound Archive has amassed a rich collection of oral history testimony, collected in partnership with the HMS *Belfast* Association. These interviews form the backbone of this book.

To locate the source of an interview quoted in these pages, search the IWM Sound Archive list by surname in the Sources section at the back of the book. The interviews are supported by a sprinkling of diaries and letters, plus the ship's log which is now deposited at the National Archives in Kew (again, full details are given in the Sources section). Illustrations have been exclusively sourced from the extraordinary IWM photograph collection – as the national repository for official wartime photographs, it contains an unparalleled body of material relating to D-Day – and from IWM's outstanding art collection, containing numerous works by official war artists who were present on D-Day and afterwards. The book is also based in part on a short article I wrote for the *Mariner's Mirror*, the journal of the Society for Nautical Research.

This is an account of D-Day as seen predominantly through the eyes of HMS *Belfast*'s crew, rather than a generic account of the landings, and as such it is at times more a series of impressions than a strictly chronological account. After more than 70 years memories can be hazy, and exact times and dates can prove elusive. Sometimes events which happened to others and have been heard second-hand can be adopted as our own memories with the passing of years, especially when we were young at the time of those events, and these men were very young. Of the men you will find in these pages, only three were older, career Royal Navy men – *Belfast*'s Captain, Senior Engineer and Torpedo Officer, who were 42, 34 and 28 years old respectively. The rest were 'Hostilities Only' ratings, civilians until a few months before. The oldest was 21 and the youngest just 18. They hailed from all over the United Kingdom, and carried out a bewildering variety of jobs aboard the complex war machine which was HMS *Belfast*. Amongst them are an Officers' Cook, a Chief Engine Room Artificer, several Seaman Gunners, an Asdic Operator, a Signaller, a Wireless Operator, a Stoker and a Radar Operator. Each of them brings a different perspective – different memories of different sights, sounds and feelings. Each of them makes up the narrative of the ship. This is their story, and hers.

CHAPTER ONE
HMS *BELFAST*, 1936–1944

'[The sea] was grey-black, death itself ... forty-foot waves,
sea temperatures below zero, ice forming on the upper
works, ice three and four inches thick that would
have to be chipped by hand.' — *Larry Fursland*

HMS *Belfast* was 'born' on 10 December 1936, in the city whose name she bore, when her keel was laid at Harland & Wolff's famous shipyard, birthplace of the *Titanic* 25 years before. An improved Southampton Class light cruiser, she had one identical sister, HMS *Edinburgh*, and eight slightly smaller half-sisters, all named after British towns (see Appendix 2 for technical specifications and a full list of Southampton Class cruisers). Launched, fittingly, on St Patrick's Day (17 March 1938) by Anne Chamberlain, wife of the prime minister, *Belfast* was commissioned into the Royal Navy on 5 August 1939, less than a month before the outbreak of the Second World War. After an early success in capturing the German blockade runner SS *Cap Norte* near the Faeroe Islands on 5 October, her first period of war service was brought to a premature end on 21 November when she detonated a German magnetic mine in the Firth of Forth whilst on her way to carry out gunnery practice. The force of the explosion broke the cruiser's back and she was very nearly scrapped. It was more than two years before she returned to service – rebuilt, and modernised with the latest equipment, including radar, new fire-control systems and 20mm Oerlikon quick-firing anti-aircraft guns. On Christmas Day 1942 she arrived at the base of the Royal Navy's Home Fleet, Scapa Flow, in the Orkney Islands, to become the flagship of Rear-Admiral Robert Burnett's 10th Cruiser Squadron. There followed a punishing 18 months operating in support of the Arctic Convoys to the Soviet Union.

Belfast's Captain, 42-year-old Frederick Parham, was an experienced veteran of three years of war in destroyers. He was a highly respected and hugely popular officer. *Belfast*'s Senior Engineer, Lieutenant-Commander Charles Simpson, described him as 'the best Captain I've ever had the pleasure to serve with ... a handsome, courteous and eventually extremely well-loved man'. Working closely with Parham was Lieutenant Andy Palmer, incorrectly rumoured to be the heir to the Huntley & Palmer biscuit fortune according to a typically wild lower-deck 'buzz'. The cruiser's Torpedo Officer, Palmer was also in charge of most of the ship's electrical systems, including those in the ship's main gun turrets, a responsibility he was himself bewildered by: 'I was a Torpedo Officer, what was I doing looking after the guns' electrics??!! Anyway that was the way it was!' As one of the cruiser's few regular officers, Palmer also had something of a mentoring role:

> When we were at sea I was one of the very few career deck officers. Most of the officers were RNVR temporary, so instead of just having an Officer

Left: 'Ice forming on the upper works, ice three and four inches thick that would have to be chipped by hand.' – Larry Fursland. Heavily muffled seamen hack the ice from HMS *Belfast*'s forecastle with shovels, hooks and crowbars, November 1943. This could be a daily activity on the Arctic run. Allowing ice to build up could threaten the ship's stability, and in extreme cases even carry a risk of her capsizing and sinking.

Left: The German blockade runner SS *Cap Norte* is boarded and captured by HMS *Belfast* on 9 October 1939 near the Faeroe Islands. The *Hamburg-Suüdamerika* liner was returning home disguised as the Swedish ship *Ancona*, laden with German reservists from South America. *Belfast*'s crew received 'prize money' for taking her. This picture was painted by the artist Harold Wyllie for Lieutenant Alan Seal, the officer who commanded the boarding party.

of the Watch on the Bridge who would be an experienced man and trained to take charge of all operations, the arrangement was ... the Officer of the Watch would be one of these temporary junior lieutenants and supervising him would be one of us long-term people who were called the principal control officer, because we would take charge of the firing of the guns as well as the navigating of the ship.

Palmer was well-placed to explain the secret behind the Captain's understated but pronounced, instinctive talent for leadership years later:

> The Captain is a fairly remote individual to a simple sailor or stoker, but in fact his influence extends throughout the ship. He doesn't have to go down around the mess decks and talk to every man, his influence is apparent all the time and Freddy Parham was a marvellous man ... he was a compassionate man ... When I damaged this aircraft on the catapult, when we got it all back to normal and the aircraft airborne and so on, I went to see Freddy Parham and said 'we can't go on like this! This is the second time I've damaged one of the aircraft. Wouldn't it better if you relieved me of this catapult work and gave somebody else the function?' But he wouldn't have it. And he didn't blame me, in fact I don't think he ever blamed me no matter what I did! That compassionate attitude would be apparent throughout the ship. Freddy Parham as either a Lieutenant-Commander or a Commander had been the Captain of a destroyer, and this had taught him a lot of compassion.

This affection was not just confined to officers. On the 'lower deck', 20-year-old Signalman Lance Tyler remembered Parham with warmth: 'Captain Parham ... he was the sort of man who would always take interest in other people ... I had a lot of time for Parham although we didn't meet very much.'

The Flag Officer in command of the 10th Cruiser Squadron was the formidable Rear-Admiral Robert Burnett. Formerly the Royal Navy's Director of Physical Training and Rear-Admiral, Home Fleet Destroyers, he further enhanced his reputation just a few days after *Belfast*'s arrival, on New Year's Eve, when he fought and won the Battle of the Barents Sea – although he chose to fly his flag in *Belfast*'s half-sister *Sheffield* on that day. Burnett was obscurely known on the lower deck as 'Nutty', and occasionally as 'Bullshit Bob' owing to his penchant for addressing his men. Following a naval tradition of patronage which Nelson would have found reassuring, the Admiral's Flag Lieutenant was his young cousin, Arthur Burnett, who recalled his cousin's strange mealtime ritual: 'he lit a cigarette and it had to be passed round all the people at the table before it came to the last person ...' Andy Palmer remembered the Admiral as 'an inveterate smoker and I could smell his cigarettes as he came up the bridge ladder. Bob was always a bit of a threat in the background ...'

By the time *Belfast* arrived at Scapa, the Arctic Convoy route to Russia via Iceland had become one of the great naval battlegrounds of the Second

Left: HMS *Belfast* after being severely damaged by a magnetic mine in the Firth of Forth, 21 November 1939. Members of the ship's company can be seen preparing life rafts on the quarter-deck and port waist, towards the aft (back) end of the ship. The explosion broke the cruiser's back and she was nearly scrapped.

World War, and the ship's first year was a busy one. Her role included convoy screening and endless duty on the Northern Patrol off Iceland, watching for attempts by enemy warships to break out into the Atlantic or for blockade runners coming in the opposite direction. The weather was arguably a greater threat than the Germans, as Captain Parham recalled:

> It is difficult to describe what conditions were like. It was of course desperately cold and in the winter desperately dark … around the shortest day, the sun never rose at all above the horizon … I was always afraid of running into solid ice … I'm reminded of the very lovely prayer … which asks God to preserve us from the dangers of the sea and the violence of the enemy in that order, and how right the writer was.

Other veterans recalled mess decks inches deep in dirty sea water and condensation, and months without mail or leave, other than brief runs ashore to the miserable rain-swept island of Flotta, the site of Scapa Flow's Fleet Cinema. Afloat, sailors made their own entertainment. Cards and 'uckers' – the Royal Navy's dog-eat-dog version of Ludo – were popular, as were model-making, boxing competitions and, perhaps bizarrely, embroidery. 'Crown and Anchor', the illegal gambling game in which vast sums were won and lost, was everywhere, despite the risk of severe punishment. George Stanley remembered games of tombola in the empty hangar formerly occupied by the ship's Walrus seaplane. Many just read everything they could get their hands on. For Boy Seaman David Jones, it was westerns: '[The Library] had 13 cowboy books and I read every one of them … I don't think I've ever read a cowboy book since.'

20-year-old Somerset-born Stoker Larry Fursland remembered how the sea 'was grey-black, death itself [with] 40 foot waves, sea temperatures below zero, ice forming on the upper works, ice three and four inches thick that would have to be chipped by hand … down below, icicles four feet long hung from the ventilation'. Some protection was provided by an issue of special Arctic clothing, but it carried hazards of its own:

> On top of our normal hard weather clothing they put the Arctic clothing … any Seaman exposed to the Arctic climate looked like a comic character. He looked as though he was walking with his head out of a tent. Now this had one terrible consequence … it was an acknowledged hazard that if a person went over … into the sea in his exposed position clothing he died within, it was estimated, four seconds.

Above: Frederick Parham, commanding officer of HMS *Belfast* from September 1942 to July 1944. Parham went on to serve as Second-in-Command of the Mediterranean Fleet (1951–52) and Fourth Sea Lord (1954–55). He finished his naval career as Commander-in-Chief, The Nore in 1955–58, and retired in 1959 as Admiral Sir Frederick Parham, GBE, KCB, DSO.

Charles Simpson

Fursland was lucky. His principal task was keeping watch over one of the ship's two diesel generators, far down below decks in the warm: 'a routine job [and] bloody noisy.'

Just making your way around the ship could be lethal for the unwary. 21-year-old seaman George Burridge, from Haslemere in Surrey, was one of *Belfast's* Radar Operators:

> To get to your place of work there were safety ropes all along the low waist of the ship, which you had to sort of clip on to and run along, otherwise there was a strong risk of being swept overboard ... It was made quite clear that if you went on the upper deck ... unless you had gloves on if you touched any part [of the ship] with your bare hand then it would just stick there.

Unlike Larry Fursland, George Burridge had a job which was multi-faceted and specialised. His principal task was to monitor the ship's Type 284 radar, a long-distance surface search set which provided the cruiser with 'eyes' which could 'see' ships out to distances of 25 miles, an enormous advantage, especially at night. But the work was exhausting:

> You sat in front of this little screen in a darkened room and you looked at this little tiny screen with a blue-and-white line across it and you were looking for what they called 'echoes', little blips on the line, and the restriction was to about 20 minutes on the set because of the strain on the eyes ... and then you changed over and then you had a little rest and then you went back.

Lance Tyler

Arthur Burnett

Left: 'It was of course desperately cold and in the winter desperately dark' – Captain Frederick Parham. November 1943: ice has formed on A and B turrets, the two forward main gun mounts. The turrets are trained at opposite angles to prevent a dangerous build-up of ice inside the gun barrel, to ensure that the guns were not damaged by the powerful Arctic waves, and to allow the ship to engage an unexpected enemy whatever direction they may appear from.

Like most of the men aboard, Burridge had more than one job. At times he had to work at the radar repeater screens in the ship's Transmitting Station – the nerve centre for *Belfast*'s big guns – hidden behind four inches of armour and buried four decks down in the bowels of the ship. Sometimes he worked in the Radar Plot Room, collating the information from all the various radars and 'plotting' the results with coloured pencils on a large chart. At times he also manned the cruiser's Type 242 IFF (Identification Friend or Foe) set, sitting for hours with headphones on in 'a little steel box just in front of the after funnel … with no ventilation and a little tiny heater', listening for signals from aircraft and identifying whether or not they were hostile. And if he had none of these duties to perform, he had to work as a normal seaman, cleaning the decks or chipping paint. Wartime service in the Royal Navy involved levels of hard work and 'multi-tasking' which would be incomprehensible to most of us today.

Convoying essential war supplies to the Soviet Union did not guarantee the sailors a warm welcome. Murmansk, the principal destination, was small, poor and only a few miles from the front line, and the local inhabitants were living in the iron grip of Stalinism. Alec Bonner recalled that 'the Russians seemed scared stiff of their superiors … you saw the odd Russian sailor, but they seemed to be scared stiff of speaking to us'.

By June 1944, then, the men of *Belfast* had already had a very tough 18 months, comprising endless sea time in foul weather with little to break up the monotony. Exceptions included the occasional sighting of an enemy aircraft, escorting Winston Churchill across the Atlantic in the liner *Queen Mary* to attend the Trident Conference in Washington in May, and on one memorable occasion loading up a cargo of Russian gold bullion (payment for the tons of war material being transferred). The grim highlight for many, however, was the Battle of North Cape, the last naval battle fought between surface ships in European waters. The German battlecruiser *Scharnhorst* had attempted to intercept outbound Arctic Convoy JW55B and homeward-bound convoy RA55A as they rounded the North Cape of Norway, just a short passage from the Kriegsmarine base at Altenfjord.

On the evening of Christmas Day 1943, *Scharnhorst* steamed from Altenfjord, her mess decks adorned with traditional Christmas decorations. She was accompanied by five large destroyers from the 4th Flotilla. The operation was codenamed 'Ostfront' and was commanded by Konteradmiral Erich Bey, an experienced officer who had commanded destroyers at the Battle of Narvik in 1940. Unknown to the Germans, the two convoys presenting themselves as tempting targets were in

George Stanley

David Jones

Larry Fursland

fact bait in an elaborate trap. British Intelligence was intercepting and deciphering German signals, and within hours the Admiralty had informed the Commander-in-Chief Home Fleet, Admiral Sir Bruce Fraser, that *Scharnhorst* was at sea, giving him plenty of time to deploy his forces. Burnett in HMS *Belfast*, with the cruisers *Norfolk* and *Sheffield*, was to screen the convoys and maintain contact with *Scharnhorst*. For the senior officers this was the opportunity they had been waiting for, and they accepted it calmly, as Captain Parham recalled:

> On the evening of Christmas Day 1943 we had a warning from the Admiralty that it was believed that the *Scharnhorst* was probably putting to sea and we were ordered to push on ahead ... and to cover another convoy which was on its way out from England and was about halfway to Murmansk. I remember very well having a long discussion with my Admiral ... in the Charthouse about what we should do ... that I think finished at about midnight.

In the engine room, Charles Simpson remembered that 'this was the job for which we'd trained, in some cases for 20 years. This was it. You now relied upon the skill of the gunners to sink the enemy before he sunk you. This was where interdepartmental co-operation was seen at its most intense. We got the gunners to the position they desired as fast as we could.'

Belfast had three states of readiness in wartime, essentially resembling a modern traffic light status system. Cruising Stations was the lowest level, equivalent to green, and Action Stations was the highest level, red. On Christmas Day 1943, the ship was at what was called Defence Stations, basically 'amber', with the ship's company manning their weapons and occupying other combat positions, but not at high alert. Larry Fursland was part of the engine room staff, and recalled how Christmas Day passed; silent, tense, everybody waiting. Finally the storm broke:

> Then came Boxing Day, St Stephen's Day, I remember as only yesterday, twenty to nine in the morning that's 08:45 Navy time. 'Action Stations' bugle! The Padre gave a short service of prayer and we all had to go to our action stations ... well my place was down the port diesel [generator], and that's where I went down and that's where I stayed for 12 hours ... Chief ERA [Engine Room Artificer] came down and started up the diesels and left me. I was clamped up each side, watertight doors, and just a hatch to go down.

George Burridge

Alec Bonner

While Burnett's 10th Cruiser Squadron screened the vulnerable merchant ships, Admiral Sir Bruce Fraser, in the battleship HMS *Duke of York*, steamed into position to the south with the cruiser HMS *Jamaica* and four destroyers, between *Scharnhorst* and her base in Norway. The trap was set. If Fraser's *Duke of York* could bring *Scharnhorst* to action, she would enjoy an overwhelming superiority in firepower, her 14-inch guns outranging and out-punching *Scharnhorst's* smaller 11-inch guns. At 07:30 on the morning of Boxing Day, the British superiority in numbers was further increased when the five large destroyers that accompanied *Scharnhorst* were ordered home. As *Scharnhorst* headed north to intercept, JW55B was 50 miles south of Bear Island, while Admiral Fraser was 200 miles away to the southwest and Admiral Burnett's cruisers were approaching the convoy from the east. First contact took place just before 09:00, when *Belfast* detected *Scharnhorst* by radar, heading south and only 30 miles east of the convoy. HMS *Norfolk* engaged and hit the battlecruiser, followed by *Belfast* and *Sheffield*. Crucially, during this action *Norfolk* disabled *Scharnhorst's* main fire control radar, leaving the German battlecruiser almost blind. She turned north and away, still trying to circle Burnett's force and reach the convoy.

Belfast had never fired a full broadside before, and some of the effects could not have been anticipated. Alone down at his action station on the port diesel generator Larry Fursland was faced with a problem; the vibration from the first broadside knocked out the two circulating pumps which cooled it. Without the generator, two triple 6-inch turrets – half *Belfast's* armament – would be out of action. Acting quickly, Fursland diverted a fire-main along the passageway above his position and down through the hatch. Without any tools, he connected it to the generator with his bare hands, bypassing the disabled pumps, and circulated salt water from the main through the generator for 12 hours. He was completely alone. For his actions Larry Fursland was later awarded the Distinguished Service Medal. The first broadside had caused another unanticipated problem on the bridge – the armoured door of the plot room had been blown off by the shockwave from *Belfast's* after turrets. For George Burridge it had a silver lining: 'for the rest of the battle we were literally able to see what was going on first hand!'

Admiral Burnett was faced with possibly the most significant decision of his career, as Captain Parham later recalled:

> The *Scharnhorst* turned north and made away at high speed, and this is where my Admiral, Burnett, had to make his really big decision, and I am

absolutely convinced it was the right one. Which was that he was not to follow the *Scharnhorst* … because we couldn't possibly have kept up. The weather was so bad that he would have probably outstripped us and would merely have got round us and probably back on to the convoy. And so my Admiral's decision was to fall back on the convoy and wait and see, I remember him saying to me 'I'll bet she'll come again'.

Burnett was absolutely correct. *Scharnhorst* returned to the convoy, only to find the 10th Cruiser Squadron once more in her path. Contact was regained at noon and all three cruisers opened fire. During the 20 minute firefight which followed, *Scharnhorst* was hit again and *Norfolk* was badly damaged by 11-inch shells. The German ship now headed south away from the convoy, attempting to return to Norway, and this time Burnett shadowed by radar. With *Norfolk* disabled and *Sheffield* suffering from engine problems, at one point *Belfast* was pursuing her formidable adversary alone. George Burridge was less than impressed by this development: 'I recall Admiral Burnett coming on and saying that we were at the moment alone and we were going to engage the *Scharnhorst*, which frightened the life out of everybody!' he remembered, '[The atmosphere] was as tense as it could be, because we knew we were in real danger then'.

The men down in the engine rooms were entirely cut off from the activity on the bridge. Without access to the upper decks, in a noisy busy environment, they simply had to carry on doing their jobs, always aware that if things went badly up above the ship might sink before they had a chance to escape. Charles Simpson recalled the tension, as every ounce of power was squeezed out of the ship's machinery for 17 hours:

It's not only the main engines, the turbines that have to go at full speed, everything that's applicable to driving the turbines has to go at full speed. So the boilers were at maximum capacity … we were kept informed, in so far as the command could allow it, of what was happening, but in order to do that in the engine rooms which were very noisy, required somebody to apply an ear to the loudspeaker. So at any crackle from the loudspeaker, indicating that it had been switched on, somebody had to go and put his ear and listen closely to what had been said, and then everyone would gather round and say 'What did he say?' [It was] tense because you knew that the ship was engaged in following the enemy … you were about to do the job for which you were employed.

It was not only the engine room personnel who had little idea about what was happening. It is sometimes hard to appreciate the lack of information available to the small cogs in the wheel – the junior officers and ratings were closed-up at action stations for hours at a time, while the action unfolded around in the total darkness of an Arctic winter. David Jones, just 18 years old, was a sight-setter and communications number, part of the crew of a twin 4-inch gun mounting:

Brian Butler

> If we went local firing, the guns were controlled by a Director Control Tower ... and the signals were sent electronically down to the gun from the Director Control Tower giving the range, bearing, elevation and all that and I just sat there and followed a dial converting an electrical pointer on a dial to a handle I used to set the fuses for the shells ... we didn't know what was going on – we were ... closed-up all the time ... I remember that I had a bacon sandwich for breakfast, an oggie [pasty] for dinner and a lump of plum duff [pudding] in the evening.

Brian Butler, another gunner confined with 26 other men in one of the ship's 6-inch turrets, recalled how, 'During lulls in the action you'd sit there with your eyes closed, there was no way you could sleep ... it was cold in the turret, it was bitterly cold in the turret'. Engine Room Artificer Ron Jesse was one of *Belfast*'s two Coppersmiths, a 'day job' which normally kept him confined to a workshop in the base of the cruiser's after funnel:

Below: 'We had quite a small periscope in the roof of the turret ... that's the only view of the outside that you would have.' – Gordon Painter.
The inside of a cruiser's 6-inch gun turret is drawn in chalks by war artist Stephen Bone, in 1944. The five men loading the left gun are wearing boiler suits and asbestos anti-flash hoods and gauntlets. Working in *Belfast*'s turrets was back-breaking, stifling and claustrophobic work.

> I had a Coppersmith's Shop I could retire to but it wasn't very pleasant. It was in the base of the after funnel ... There were a couple of us Coppersmiths and there was a Blacksmith and the Blacksmith had been on the ship a long time before me and he knew it all, he was a much older man

and I was a boy of 19, and he ruled the roost in this shop with two forges and two benches and two anvils, one for him and one for us.

In normal circumstances, Jesse's job was not very different to equivalent roles in civilian life. At 08:00 he joined a queue, and was assigned work from the 'job book' by Charles Simpson, 'a bright, sharp little man ... very jovial, very pleasant but very sharp'. Jesse then had to go and find whatever was causing the trouble amongst the bewildering maze of pipework running the length and breadth of HMS *Belfast*, and fix the problem, which was invariably a leak. Alternatively he might spend the day in his workshop, repairing pipes which had already been removed. But in action everything changed. One of Jesse's action stations was deep inside the ship, standing by a set of valves which would if necessary allow sea water into B Turret's magazines and shell rooms: 'To save the magazine exploding I had to flood it and drown everybody down there, that was my action station. I took the locks off the ... hand wheels on the deck outside the turret and stood there ready to do that.' Isolated and alone, his experience of combat was characterised by uncertainty: 'The bangs started and we worked up to full speed and the bangs went on and the shudders and the bangs and then it all died away and the Commander said "she's made off".'

It is easy to imagine how these circumstances might induce fear, although in reality the battle was going well. By now Admiral Fraser in *Duke of York* was to the south-southwest, ideally placed to cut off *Scharnhorst*'s retreat. Fraser made radar contact soon after 16:00 at a range of 22 miles and closed in. At 16:50 *Belfast* illuminated *Scharnhorst* with starshell, and Burnett's cruisers engaged from one side while *Duke of York* and *Jamaica* opened fire from the other. *Duke of York* hit *Scharnhorst* with her first salvo and swiftly began to inflict severe damage. 19-year-old Bob 'Ping' Shrimpton, from Fleet in Hampshire, was *Belfast*'s 'Asdic' (today called Sonar) Operator. The sensitive submarine detection equipment was unusable in the frantic high-speed manoeuvring of a surface action; instead he was able to creep up on deck and witness *Scharnhorst*'s death throws:

> Once the Duke of York got in there, with those tremendous guns, it was horrendous to watch ... they just smashed the thing to pieces ... it was just one blaze from one end to the other ... You could see these flashes in the darkness coming through and you could watch the fall of shot as it lit up ... we closed as close as possible so that we could open fire on it ... her guns kept firing, just before she went down.

Ronald Jesse

Gradually the German ship's guns were put out of action, and her superstructure reduced to a twisted mass of burning steel. Then, a shell from *Duke of York* penetrated a boiler room and severed a steam pipe, reducing *Scharnhorst's* speed to ten knots. Bey sent his last signal to his superiors: 'We shall fight to the last shell'. By now, according to all eyewitnesses, his ship was ablaze from stem to stern. Fraser seized his chance, and ordered his destroyers to close in to point-blank range and attack with torpedoes. Four found their targets, leaving *Scharnhorst* dead in the water and a sitting target as *Duke of York* and the cruisers opened fire again.

At 19:45 HMS *Belfast* was ordered in to deliver the *coup de grace* to *Scharnhorst* with Andy Palmer's torpedoes. Years later he described the moment:

Bob Shrimpton

> We swung the ship and fired the starboard torpedoes and I said to Captain Parham, 'swing her back the other way and we'll fire the other salvo', but by the time we got the ship swinging somehow or other the *Norfolk* had crept up … and I would have torpedoed her so I had to say 'I'm sorry she's fouled the range'. So we turned round and then when we turned back again the flames had gone out and she's sunk … I was so certain that we'd got a hit that I had a swastika painted on to that particular tube.

In fact, as *Belfast* turned a tremendous explosion had ripped through the German ship, probably originating from her forward magazines. She rapidly began to settle and at 19:48, as Palmer fired, her radar blip vanished, to be followed by a series of muffled underwater explosions. The initial reaction aboard *Belfast* was one of elation but as the full enormity of loss of life became apparent this was soon replaced by more sombre feelings. All that could be seen were a pitifully small number of red lifejacket lights, each representing a man fighting for his life in the oil-covered water. Bob Shrimpton remembered a moment of dead silence, when 'a lot of people were thinking there's a hell of a lot of men on there the same as us, youngsters, families, wives, kids, and they're in that water. I think that was a subduing effect'. Even in the engine room, the unmistakeable stench of oil fuel came down through the ventilation shafts, reaching Charles Simpson and his men: 'I was so overcome with pity for those Germans swimming about in oil fuel that I had no other feeling than pity for several minutes … I don't think I felt like cheering … the job had been accomplished.'

Just 36 survivors were rescued before the British ships were ordered to vacate the area due to the danger of attack by U-boats. 1,927 men died. British dead numbered 18, on board *Norfolk* and the destroyer *Saumarez*, but the completeness of the victory could not be denied. As the triumphant *Belfast* made her way to Murmansk Captain Parham ordered 'spice the mainbrace', and extra rum was distributed to all. The ship's company were very aware of the importance of their achievement. With the destruction of *Scharnhorst* any hopes the Germans had of mounting a serious surface threat to the Russian convoys effectively evaporated. George Stanley remembered *Belfast*'s triumphant return to Scapa on New Year's Day, 1944:

> All the ships were lined up as we came through, fantastic, cheers, you know ... we got leave just after that ... and I came home ... we went to a pub ... and my sister told some of the people that I'd just come off the *Belfast* and they had me up on the stage. I didn't know what I was doing because I think I was drunk.

For their successful command of the battle, Fraser was later made the first Baron Fraser of North Cape, and Burnett was knighted. As for *Belfast*, her Captain, Frederick Parham, received the Distinguished Service Order. He also received a personal tribute from his friend and the former C-in-C Home Fleet, Lord Tovey, who wrote: 'The combination of the gallant attack you and the other cruisers made on the *Scharnhorst*, coupled with your magnificent shadowing, is as fine an example of cruiser work as has ever been seen.'

After North Cape, life was relatively quiet for *Belfast* and her crew. Apart from providing distant cover for Operation 'Tungsten' – an aircraft-carrier strike against the German battleship *Tirpitz* in her lair at Altenfjord – the cruiser spent the winter at Scapa Flow or Rosyth. Then on 17 April 1944 she was sent to the Clyde for a refit. There was a sense that something major was in the offing, although at this stage nobody on board had been officially told that it was Operation 'Overlord'. Had they been, it was unlikely there would have been much apprehension. *Belfast* was now a veteran. Her systems, machinery and crew had been honed by 18 months of gruelling Arctic service, and sharpened by a successful action against a courageous and experienced foe. *Belfast* and her men were ready.

CHAPTER TWO
OPERATION 'OVERLORD'

'We went into the Clyde and we saw all these landing craft everywhere and we said what are those 'cos we'd never seen one before.' — *Bob Shrimpton*

Belfast, like most ships and military units, was coming late to a party that had been a long time in the planning. British thoughts of returning an army to continental Europe to engage and defeat the Germans began almost immediately after the disastrous Battle for France in the summer of 1940 and the British Expeditionary Force's remarkable, but nevertheless ignominious, escape across the beaches of Dunkirk into the welcome embrace of Royal Navy warships and the famous 'little ships' between 27 May and 4 June. But these were pipe dreams – Britain lacked the troops and the resources required to cross the channel, and for the first year it was as much as she could do to simply survive.

After Hitler's catastrophic decision to invade Russia in June 1941, British survival became more likely. The British Empire and the Communist Soviet Union became unlikely allies, Winston Churchill famously remarking that 'if Hitler invaded Hell, I would at least make a favourable reference to the Devil in the House of Commons'. The Soviet dictator, Joseph Stalin, immediately began to push for the opening of an offensive against the Germans in the west to take pressure off the hard-pressed Red Army. He was supported by British Communist 'fellow travellers', creeping out after dark to daub 'Second Front Now' on walls the length and breadth of the United Kingdom, but neither they nor Stalin had any real understanding of sea warfare or the challenges posed and risks inherent in such an undertaking. Britain was still not capable of a cross-channel invasion. Instead, the British fought on the periphery – in the North African desert, first against Germany's Italian allies and later General Erwin Rommel's legendary Afrika Korps; in the skies over Germany through a strategic bombing offensive of ever increasing ferocity; and, of course, at sea, whilst supplying the Russians with whatever war material the Empire could spare, much of it sent via the perilous Arctic route which *Belfast*'s men had learned to loathe so much. Then, on 7 December 1941, Japan attacked without warning Pearl Harbor, Hawaii, the principal base of the United States Pacific Fleet. Four days later, Adolf Hitler made a second disastrous decision when he declared war on the USA. Britain had a new ally, one with almost limitless industrial and military potential. Serious planning for a return to Europe began.

At the Arcadia conference, held in Washington DC on 31 December 1941, the new allies confirmed a key strategic principal – the priority would be to defeat Germany. For the US president, Franklin Roosevelt, this was a controversial and politically sensitive decision, given that it was Japan and not Germany which had attacked the USA without provocation.

Left: 'Some of these [ships] had barrage balloons up to stop the German aircraft attacking too low.' – Gordon Painter. Camouflaged LCTs exercising in the Solent before D-Day. The barrage balloons were fitted to deter German dive bombers, a lesson learned during years of bitter fighting in the Mediterranean earlier in the war. In reality, the air threat off Normandy was much reduced, and mainly involved high-level bombing by night rather than dive bombing by day.

From the very beginning, therefore, the Americans were in a hurry to defeat Germany and then turn the full weight of their overwhelming military force towards the Pacific. The British, scarred by Dunkirk and years of setbacks against the Germans in North Africa, wanted to wait. Churchill in particular was uncharacteristically cautious, haunted by his disastrous amphibious campaign at Gallipoli nearly 30 years before. 'Why are we trying to do this', he once despairingly said, 'I am very uneasy about the whole operation'.

There followed two years of strategic cat-and-mouse, as the United States gradually replaced Great Britain as the senior partner in what became known as the Grand Alliance – the sheer latent strength of the superpower-in-waiting overwhelming British experience and political guile. Meanwhile, in the east, the Red Army recovered and began gradually to grind down the fighting power of the German armed forces on a front spanning thousands of miles. Contrary to popular mythology, the Second World War did not escape the ghastly attritional battles and trench warfare which characterised the First World War; they were just fought in the east, not in the west.

Almost immediately, the Americans began building up forces in Great Britain ready for a cross-channel invasion, a process which was codenamed 'Bolero'. The first invasion plan, optimistically codenamed Operation 'Roundup', was scheduled to take place no later than April 1943. The British, convinced that the time was not right, instead persuaded their ally to embark on a series of operations in the Mediterranean, the first aimed at ending the North African campaign through Operation 'Torch' – the invasion of Morocco and Tunisia in November 1942. Then, at the Casablanca Conference (codenamed Symbol) in January 1943, the British managed to extend these operations into a full-blown campaign to knock Italy out of the war, through the invasion of first Sicily (Operation 'Husky') in July 1943, then the Italian mainland at Salerno (Operation 'Avalanche') in September 1943, and finally the secondary landing at Anzio to try and unlock the bitter stalemate into which the Italian campaign had descended (Operation 'Shingle') in January 1944.

The Americans were fully aware that they had been 'suckered' into accepting a British peripheral strategy at Casablanca, and entered 1943 determined not to be outplayed again. At the Trident conference in Washington in May 1943, they forced the British to accept that the invasion of Northwest Europe, now codenamed 'Overlord', would take place on 1 May 1944. At Tehran in November/December 1943, the date

Left: 'All these barges full of soldiers' – Len Beardsley. A British Landing Craft Tank (LCT), laden with soldiers and American-built M4 Sherman tanks, at an English south coast port before D-Day. The vehicles have been protected with waterproofing at vulnerable points, including around the gun barrels. The soldiers' relaxed demeanour indicates this was probably an exercise.

was confirmed with Stalin. Despite continued British objections, 1944 was definitely going to be the year.

There are many excellent and very detailed publications about Anglo-American grand strategy during the Second World War, including the build-up to Operation 'Overlord'. For the present book, it is acceptable to simply consider a few points. Poor performance in the field at the Battle of Kasserine Pass and elsewhere in North Africa indicates that the US Army was almost certainly not ready to fight the Germans in 1943. The 'Bolero' build-up took longer than anticipated, and the overwhelming Allied strength which existed in the spring of 1944 simply did not exist the year before. Furthermore, Germany was undoubtedly weaker after another year of war against the Soviet Union. The operations in the Mediterranean, whilst perhaps of questionable strategic worth, had not been wholly wasted; three major assault landings had taught the Allies priceless lessons about tactics, and enabled them to develop the invaluable specialised equipment which characterised D-Day. By June 1944 the Allied sea, air and land forces were at a peak of efficiency and strength, and it is hard to visualise how they could have been any better prepared for the task in front of them.

Detailed planning for D-Day began with the appointment of Lieutenant-General Frederick Morgan as COSSAC – Chief of Staff to the Supreme Allied Commander – in May 1943, although no Supreme Commander would be in post until the end of the year. Morgan and his small team scoured the coast of occupied Europe for an appropriate location for landing an invasion force. Photographic reconnaissance aircraft swept low over beaches from northern Norway to the Franco–Spanish border, scattering surprised German soldiers in their wake. An appeal was announced in Britain for pre-war holiday photographs and postcards from any European coastal location. Millions were gathered. Largely uncatalogued and unsorted, hundreds of thousands still survive in the IWM collections. Later, Royal Navy and British Army commandoes from the Combined Operations Pilotage Parties, known as COPPists, swam ashore and took samples from the beaches. On New Year's Eve 1943, Major Logan Scott-Bowden crept ashore at Luc-sur-Mer, a section of which would one day go down in history as Gold beach. He spent hours in occupied France, taking measurements and sand samples: 'As we swam back through heavy surf towards our rendezvous point I thought my companion was in trouble when I heard him shouting. But when I turned to help, he only wished me "A Happy New Year". I told him to "swim you b*****, or we'll land back on the beach"'.

Right: Aerial reconnaissance photograph showing startled German troops taking cover from a low-flying Allied aircraft after it has surprised them in the act of erecting beach obstacles – a mixture of stakes, Czech hedgehogs (metal defences) and ramps. What seems to be some sort of small military vehicle is parked on the beach. Thousands of detailed aerial photographs like this were obtained in the months before D-Day, often at great risk to the pilots responsible for taking them.

Far right: Royal Navy Commandos prepare to demolish Czech hedgehogs, at La Rivière after D-Day. Hundreds of thousands of extra obstacles had been ordered by Field Marshal Erwin Rommel after he inspected German defences in north-west Europe at the end of 1943. The lack of preparedness and complacency that he found when he began his tour in Denmark on 30 November had appalled him.

Two weeks later, Scott-Bowden returned to Normandy aboard the Royal Navy midget submarine *X-20*, this time to survey the American sector. When *X-20* first reached the target area, her commanding officer, Lieutenant Ken Hudspeth, surfaced in the midst of a French fishing fleet. Scott-Bowden raised the periscope, only to look right into the eyes of a bored German soldier perched on the stern of a fishing boat, presumably a sentry posted to discourage the fishermen from heading across the Channel to join the Free French. With characteristic understatement, Scott-Bowden pronounced himself 'a little surprised', and downed periscope 'pretty smartly'.

To avoid giving German intelligence any clues to the actual invasion site, obvious planning measures, including aircraft overflights and appeals for holiday snaps, had to encompass almost the entire European coastline. But in reality Allied options were quite limited: 'The limiting factors for an invasion site were the radius of air cover (effectively the range of a Spitfire, 150 miles); the limits of beach capacity (it was scarcely possible to unload an army beneath steep cliffs); the length of the sea crossing; and the strength of the German defences'.

These limitations ruled out most of Europe. Norway and Denmark were too far away, as was the southwest French coast along the Bay of Biscay. Even Brittany lay outside the reach of air cover. Holland was characterised by appalling terrain in which to fight a battle, low lying and easy for the Germans to deliberately flood. The shortest crossing, across the Straits of Dover to the Pas de Calais, was as obvious to the Germans as it was to the Allies and was consequently too strongly defended. The Cotentin Peninsula was near enough, and offered the tempting port of Cherbourg on its tip. Keeping the army in France supplied and reinforced (and thus for Operation 'Overlord' to succeed), capturing a large, functioning port seemed vital. But the Cotentin was eventually rejected; it would be too easy for the Germans to establish a strong defence line across the base of the peninsula, potentially keeping the Allies bottled-up indefinitely. As early as the summer of 1943, the COSSAC planners thus settled on a 50-mile stretch of Normandy coastline fronting on to the Baie-de-la-Seine. Detailed planning now focussed on this area, although deception operations continued to encourage the Germans to believe the attack might come anywhere; Hitler himself still believed an invasion of Norway was the most likely threat, and hundreds of thousands of German troops remained in that country until the end of the war.

The main features of the final 'Overlord' plan were to put ashore, after a heavy naval and air bombardment, three US divisions, two British divisions and one Canadian infantry division on five beaches, supported by special service troops (British Commandos and US Rangers), specialised tanks and other armoured vehicles and, eventually, a bewildering array of support troops. The codenames for the invasion beaches are today almost as famous as D-Day itself: Omaha and Utah (US); Sword and Gold (British) and Juno (Canadian). Three divisions of paratroops – around 20,000 men – would be dropped to protect the British left and US right flanks. Once the beachhead had been secured, follow-up forces would be landed at a rate of just over one extra division a day.

On 7 December 1943, US General Dwight David Eisenhower was appointed as Supreme Commander and began to establish a headquarters known as SHAEF (Supreme Headquarters Allied Expeditionary Forces). Reflecting the sensitivities of alliance politics, Eisenhower's key deputies were all British, and it is fair to say that Eisenhower's appointment owed more to his qualities as diplomat and peacemaker, what one author has called his 'extraordinary generosity of spirit', than to his abilities as a field commander.

Eisenhower's Deputy Supreme Commander was Air Chief Marshal Sir Arthur Tedder, an unmistakeable indication of the importance air power would play in the coming campaign. Ground forces for the invasion would all fall under the British 21st Army Group, commanded by General Sir Bernard Montgomery, better known as 'Monty', hero of the desert war and victor of El Alamein, the only major land battle won by British

Empire forces alone. The Allied air forces would be commanded by Air Chief Marshal Sir Trafford Leigh Mallory.

It was almost inevitable that the predominantly British naval forces were under the command of a British admiral – the experienced and highly respected Admiral Sir Bertram Ramsay. On the point of retirement before the outbreak of war, Ramsay had been recalled to active duty in time to mastermind Operation 'Dynamo', the evacuation from Dunkirk, in 1940. He had already played a pivotal role in the landings in North Africa and Sicily, and was the obvious choice to take charge of Operation 'Neptune'. Ramsey's final plan as issued to his commanders ran to more than 700 pages, a 3-inch thick masterpiece of detailed planning, more than enough to weaken the resolve of Parham and his fellow captains. William Donald, commanding officer of HMS *Ulster*, was an experienced combat veteran who had been serving continuously at sea since 1939. In his best-selling autobiography, *Stand By For Action*, published in 1975, he wrote:

Above: Aerial view of Nan Green Beach, Juno Area, east of the River Seulles at Courseulles-sur-Mer. The beach is strewn with stakes and Czech hedgehogs, and in the centre the white scar of *Widerstandsnest* (resistance post) 29 can be clearly seen. This position was captured by the Regina Rifles and the 1st Hussars of 7th Canadian Brigade, after heavy fighting on 6 June, when HMS *Belfast* was operating off this area.

Above: D-Day's senior Allied commanders meeting in London on 1 February 1944. Left to right, front row: Air Chief Marshal Sir Arthur W. Tedder, Deputy Supreme Commander; General Dwight Eisenhower, Supreme Commander; General Sir Bernard Montgomery, Commander in Chief, 21st Army Group; back row: Lieutenant General Omar Bradley, Commander-in-Chief, US 1st Army; Admiral Sir Bertram Ramsay, Allied Naval Commander-in-Chief, Expeditionary Force; Air Chief Marshal Sir Trafford Leigh-Mallory, Allied Air Commander-in-Chief; and Lieutenant General Walter Bedell-Smith, Eisenhower's Chief-of-Staff.

Above: 'Admiral Ramsay was a marvellous man. We knew every ship ... everybody knew exactly where to go and anchor, and exactly when to open fire.' — Captain Frederick Parham. Admiral Sir Bertram Ramsay, KCB, KBE, CB, MVO (the mastermind of Operation 'Neptune'), and Rear-Admiral Alan G Kirk, USN (responsible for the American beaches), aboard the minelayer HMS *Apollo* on 7 June 1944. Ramsay was killed in an air crash on 2 January 1945, whilst flying to a conference in Brussels.

If the orders for the Anzio landing had been considerable, those for 'Overlord' were ten times as comprehensive. In addition to the main file of overall instructions, there were half a dozen other sealed envelopes with details of all the 'sidelines'. I put them aside and started working through the main file. After an hour or so, when I had started to hoist in some of the salient points, I noticed another envelope labelled 'Corrections and Addenda'. So I had to get a pen and ink and start again. By midday I was quite exhausted, and also not a little worried. For the orders were all 'For Commanding Officer Only', and it did not seem humanly possible for one man to deal with the vast amount of corrections, chart preparation and so on.

Ramsey himself later wrote: 'That the operation proceeded smoothly and according to plan was the result of the hard work and the foresight of many thousands concerned in its preparation and of the determination and courage of tens of thousands in the Allied navies and merchant fleets who carried out their orders in accordance with the very highest traditions of the sea'.

Under Ramsay were the two Naval Task Force commanders. The Eastern Naval Task Force, responsible for the British and Canadian beaches of Sword, Juno and Gold, was under the command of Rear-Admiral Sir Phillip Vian RN, famous for his exploits in command of the

Left: 'That the operation proceeded smoothly ... was the result of the hard work and the foresight of many thousands concerned in its preparation.' – Admiral Sir Bertram Ramsay. An unidentified 'Wren' mechanic from the Women's Royal Naval Service (WRNS), welding on the deck of a landing craft before D-Day. Women may not have landed on the beaches on 6 June 1944, but they contributed to the success of the D-Day landings in countless vital and often unsung ways.

Left: 'If you looked across from the Isle of Wight you could have walked across to France on ships and landing craft!' – Joseph Stagno.
A vast Allied invasion convoy assembling off the Isle of Wight before D-Day, June 1944. Every conceivable type of ship can be picked out, from tugs and small warships to large transports and, of course, landing craft of all sizes and descriptions.

destroyer *Cossack* at the beginning of the war. In command of the Western Naval Task Force and responsible for the American beaches Omaha and Utah was Rear-Admiral Alan G Kirk USN, a former Director of Naval Intelligence. Both Vian and Kirk had already experienced the complexities of senior command during an amphibious landing, at Sicily and Salerno. This was a veteran command team.

Under the Task Force commanders were the five assault forces, each with a letter code corresponding to the first letter of the beach which they were assigned to. Two further forces, codenamed B and L, landed the follow-up troops. The assault forces were equipped with a mass of specialised vessels, mostly variations on the ubiquitous landing craft. If the Royal Navy had learned anything at all from the disastrous landings at Gallipoli in 1915 (carried out using open ships' rowing boats and an old collier, the *River Clyde*, converted into an improvised death-trap of an assault ship), it was the importance of building specialised assault shipping.

Belfast's crew could expect to be exposed to a bewildering array of specialist craft. Had the ship spent any time in the Mediterranean they might well have been familiar with at least some of them, but none of them would have made an appearance on the Arctic Convoys. Some experts have identified as many as 60 different types of landing craft used in Operation 'Overlord'.

The military designations for these craft were cumbersome and largely impenetrable acronyms: LCT, LCVP, LCA, LST, LCG. By far the biggest were the LSTs, or Landing Ships (Tank). The British first deployed tank landing ships in the Mediterranean, hastily converting three oil tankers into crude assault ships able to carry 18 Churchill tanks. By 'Overlord' they had evolved into 4,080 ton ocean-going ships with a flat forward end and massive clamshell doors which opened to let down a ramp, across which tanks and other vehicles could rumble. Once empty, the LST could either float clear on the next high tide or winch itself off using stern anchors. Although LSTs had the enormous advantage of being able to discharge cargo straight on to the beach, they were huge slab-sided ships, slow and unarmoured. Nicknamed 'Large Slow Targets' by the sailors who manned them, they were too vulnerable to be used in the first wave, when they would be an obvious target for enemy gunners. There were never enough LSTs to meet every requirement, and it is remarkable how often Allied grand strategy turned on the need to shuffle small numbers of these ugly, unglamorous workhorses halfway around the world.

At the other end of the scale were tiny infantry landing craft, the British-designed and built Landing Craft (Assault), and the famous American Landing Craft (Vehicle and Personnel), originally conceived as workboats (and sometimes 'rum runners' during the Prohibition era) for the swampy inshore waters of Louisiana. Designed by Andrew Higgins of New Orleans, they became known to history as the Higgins Boat. Each craft could carry a platoon of fully equipped infantry straight into battle. In between were literally dozens of other specialist types, each carefully designed to fulfil a specific function. Most numerous were the Landing Craft (Tank), scaled-up versions of an assault craft which still essentially resembled an overgrown steel shoebox, with rudimentary machinery spaces and crew accommodation crammed in aft. More than eight hundred LCTs took part in 'Overlord', each capable of carrying ten tanks or other heavy vehicles into battle.

Some LCTs were adapted to provide close-range fire support to the invading soldiers, without risking warships – in short supply, these were costly assets to jeopardise unnecessarily. Perhaps the most memorable for participants in 'Overlord' were the extraordinary Landing Craft Tank (Rocket), which would plaster the beaches with over 1,000 5-inch explosive rockets immediately before the landings, although according to some sources their actual impact did not live up to the undoubtedly terrifying visual impression they made. Despite the noise and pyrotechnics

Right: LCG (Medium) underway. LCG (M) type craft were designed to go close to the shore, where they would flood down until they were actually resting on the bottom to make as stable a gun platform as possible. They were armed with Army pattern 25-pounder (88mm) or 17-pounder (76mm) guns in single turrets. The ship shown here, LCG (M) 102, is armed with 25-pounders.

Far right: The Commanding Officer (lower berth) and First Lieutenant in their tiny cabin aboard an LCT. Service in landing craft was inevitably rather less formal than aboard a major warship like HMS *Belfast,* and much less comfortable – landing craft crews received an additional allowance known as 'hard lying money' as compensation. The original caption rather prissily invites the viewer to 'note photographs of film actresses pinned to the bunk'!

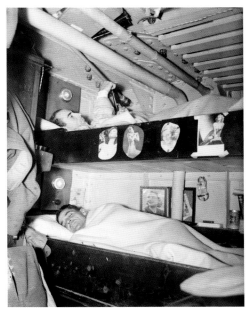

which accompanied their firings, they were inaccurate and took as long as six hours to reload. More effective were the Landing Craft Gun, LCTs turned into small warships with the addition of two 4.7-inch naval guns or a pair of Army 25-pounder gun-howitzers and Oerlikon quick-firers mounted on a false deck built over the tank hold. Landing Craft (Flak) carried anti-aircraft guns to fend off a threat from the Luftwaffe, which ultimately proved illusory. Other specialist ships were less martial in their function, like the Landing Barge (Kitchen) and Landing Barge (Bakery), designed to provide catering services afloat to the thousands of soldiers and sailors marooned in tiny assault craft with little or no onboard facilities. Still others provided floating repair or medical facilities. Even humble Thames lighters were renamed 'Landing Barge (Vehicle) and pressed into service. Sub-Lieutenant Peter Bird commanded one:

> When the Americans came into the war we got possibly 1,000 Chrysler marine engines and they decided to convert these 'dumb' lighters. They put a ramp in the stern, a watertight bulkhead, twin Chrysler marine engines and a steering wheelhouse box thing on the starboard side, aft, and, of course, a rudder for steering the vessel. Most of the coxswains were ex-Thames Lightermen ... some ... were as old as my father but they were all jolly good types and I got on with them very well.

Top left: Close up of the 4·7-inch (120mm) gun and crew aboard a Landing Craft Gun (Large). LCGs were converted from tank landing craft by building a false deck over the hold. They provided heavy gunfire to support the troops ashore without risking valuable ships like destroyers or HMS *Belfast* close inshore, where they were vulnerable to enemy attack and unable to manoeuvre. The guns were removed from destroyers to make way for anti-submarine weapons.

Bottom left: 'We supply every day and in all weathers, hot meals for 500 to 700 men.' — 19-year-old Midshipman J S Mcintyre RNVR, commanding officer of a Landing Barge Kitchen (LBK), interviewed for *The War Illustrated* in September 1944. Here, small landing craft tie up alongside an LBK so their crews can join the queue for a hot midday meal. Cooking facilities aboard the assault craft were almost non-existent, and the LBKs, another Thames dumb lighter conversion, performed a vital role.

Above: 'Landing craft of all varieties' – Charles Bunbury.

A Landing Barge Emergency Repair in 1943. These were converted Thames 'dumb' (unpowered) barges, fitted out with workshops to repair landing craft and minor warships. Designed to be towed across the Channel and then anchored, they were an excellent example of the attention to detail which characterised Normandy. Years of experience in the Mediterranean had taught invasion planners that the fleet had to take everything it needed with it.

Complementing ships designed to ground themselves intentionally were vehicles which could swim, another vital weapon in the arsenal of the Allied amphibious warfare machine. As well as the famous DUKWs, or 'Ducks', which were essentially standard GMC six-wheeled military trucks with a watertight hull and a propeller, miniature 'Ducks' were designed using similarly adapted jeeps. DUKW was not intended to sound like 'Duck'. It was in fact GMC corporate code – D for 1942, the year of manufacture; U for utility vehicle; K for all-wheel drive; W for two powered rear axles. The British also developed Duplex Drive (DD) swimming tanks, fitted with a rubberised canvas flotation screen and an ingenious secondary drive system attached to a propeller to allow them to travel through the water at four knots, or 4.6 miles per hour. Other specialist tanks were developed to clear mines and beach obstacles, remove wrecked vehicles and bridge ditches, amongst other purposes. Collectively, they were nicknamed 'Hobart's Funnies', after the messianic visionary Major-General Sir Percy Hobart, commanding officer of the 79th Armoured Division, which operated much of this equipment.

With the first assault wave would travel the Corncobs, worn-out ships which would either be towed across to Normandy, or make one last journey under their own power, before being scuttled, at which point they would be redesignated as breakwaters known as Gooseberries.

Left: The remarkable Sherman DD (Dupex Drive) swimming tank. When in the water the partially collapsed flotation screen seen here was fully raised to form a canvas box which allowed the tank to float, and engine power was shifted from the tracks to two propellers at the rear, which moved it through the water at a speed of 4 knots (7 kilometres) per hour. At D-Day DD tanks were deployed from LCTs, about 2 miles offshore.

Left: Giants' Building Blocks: Tugs towing a massive Phoenix breakwater across the Channel to form part of the Mulberry harbour. The Phoenix units were sunk in a line to replace the Gooseberry blockships with a more effective breakwater, once the fighting had moved inland and the immediate area of the beachhead was safer. They were hollow – passage crews travelled across with them, including an anti-aircraft gun and crew which can be seen on top.

These would provide a degree of shelter for the vulnerable landing craft until the completion of the more substantial Mulberry harbours. These miracles of engineering were assembled from hundreds of prefabricated steel and concrete sections, manufactured in turn by more than 300 companies all over the United Kingdom. The principal components justify a brief summary here. The main, outer breakwaters were formed from enormous caissons which could be flooded until they rested on the sea bed. Codenamed Phoenix, the largest of them displaced more than 6,000 tons, and their remains can still be seen protruding from the placid waters off Arromanches like a giant's building blocks. Outside the Phoenix and Gooseberry barrier was an outer breakwater, formed of floating cruciform steel structures known as Bombardons. Spuds were pier heads with four steel legs which could attach to the sea bed, rather like an oil rig, and were connected to the shore by floating roadways known as Whales, supported on pontoons called Beetles. The entire Mulberry structure was held in place by 2,000 ingenious anchors known as Kites.

Above: A Spud pierhead unit waiting to be towed to Normandy. Spuds were massive floating barges that could slide up and down on four adjustable posts. These went through the steel hull and anchored in the harbour bottom, enabling the piers to rise and fall with the tide, keeping the surface level and steady. Below decks, the Spuds housed generators, winches and a maintenance shop, as well as a galley and living quarters for the crew.

Rather than organise the entire invasion around the need to capture a port, a process which had been proved to be risky to the point of unachievable by the disastrous Dieppe Raid in 1942, the D-Day planners had thus decided to take their port with them. Two Mulberry harbours were built, Mulberry A at St-Laurent-sur-Mer to service the American sector and Mulberry B at Arromanches for the British. The sites were meticulously surveyed in early 1944 by the Royal Navy's 712th Survey Flotilla, whose personnel made repeated, dangerous covert trips across the Channel in converted landing craft.

Supporting the assault forces were the bombardment forces to carry out fire support, counter battery fire against gun emplacements ashore, and protect the invasion fleet from attack by the German warships based in the Channel Ports. These included 6 battleships, 19 cruisers and nearly 100 destroyers. Deployed to clear a way through the English Channel fields would be 189 minesweepers, leaving rows of lighted buoys to guide the fleet through ten swept channels. HMS *Belfast* would be the flagship of Bombardment Force E, part of Vian's Eastern Naval Task Force, and would be providing support to the Canadians at Juno (see Appendix 3 for a list of ships in Bombardment Force E.) For this important task a new admiral would be coming aboard. Rear-Admiral Frederick Dalrymple-Hamilton, the scion of an old Scottish aristocratic family, was according to Parham, 'another very very charming man'. He was an experienced fighting sailor, having served throughout the First World War, and more recently had commanded the battleship HMS *Rodney* when she helped to sink the German battleship *Bismarck* in May 1941. As well as *Belfast*, Dalrymple-Hamilton would have under his command the cruiser *Diadem*, and nine destroyers, most of them British but also including one Norwegian, one Free French and two Canadian ships. *Belfast* had been assigned her place in the vast, complex machine that was Operation 'Neptune', months before anyone aboard the ship knew anything about it.

CHAPTER THREE
WARNING SIGNS

'We still weren't told officially that D-Day was starting, [but] we left and all the dockyard maties standing on the quayside cheering away, they all knew!' — *Leslie Coleman*

For most of the ship's company, *Belfast*'s D-Day story began in early May, when the cruiser entered Rosyth Dockyard for a speedy refit to make good the damage caused by the rigours of Arctic service and to update vital equipment. Although the exact location and timing of Operation 'Overlord' was a closely guarded secret, the imminence of the 'Second Front' and the enormous build-up of men, supplies and equipment could not possibly be hidden from watching eyes on both sides of the English Channel. For some, including Asdic Operator Bob Shrimpton, there was a welcome opportunity for a brief rest: 'I managed to get just under a week's leave ... at home. I managed to get a travel warrant ... it was a great break ... It was a time we relaxed from the incessant movement of the ship and the incessant changing of watches, you could relax but then you had to key yourself back aboard again.' Adjusting to domestic routine after months at sea was not easy: 'It's more difficult to wind down! I remember coming home and I'd go to bed at 12 o' clock at night [and] I'd be waking up at 4, it was that mental habit that you got into. At 8 o'clock in the morning I'd want to go and have a lie down.'

Leslie Coleman

Coppersmith Ron Jesse had to stay on board, but he did get a chance for local leave ashore where he took up dancing classes and going to the theatre, both new experiences for him. The appeal of such pursuits was doubtless heightened by the opportunity they offered 'to get to know one or two girls which I hadn't had the opportunity to do up to then ... !' Most of the time though Jesse remembered simply sheer hard graft, advising dockyard workers on the practical performance of the ship in real combat conditions, and helping to make modifications based on his experience trying to operate and maintain her machinery in the Arctic:

> I also did a lot of improvement work myself ... like putting valve spindles up through armoured decks so that we could work the engines from above decks so that there need be nobody in the engine room. We could work all the valves [in an] emergency from above the decks, which meant taking all the valve spindles up thought the decks [and] drilling quite large holes with rudimentary ratchet drills. That's the sort of work I got up to and I quite enjoyed that experience.

21-year-old Ordinary Seaman Leslie Coleman remembered a telling sign on the day *Belfast* departed Rosyth. In typical fashion, the dockyard rumour mill seemed to mean that those ashore were probably better informed than those afloat: 'we still weren't told officially that D-Day

Left: 'Nobody knew where or when but everybody knew what we were off to do and it was an atmosphere of high excitement.' – Charles Bunbury. Resplendent in her Admiralty Disruptive Camouflage scheme, HMS *Belfast* departs Scapa Flow for the Normandy beaches, 30 May 1944. She stopped briefly on the Clyde on the way to take on extra stores and ammunition.

was starting, [but] we left and all the dockyard maties standing on the quayside cheering away, they all knew!'

Wireless Operator Len Beardsley was responsible for monitoring a constant flow of signals traffic coming in on the Admiralty band:

> [I was] mainly listening to the Admiralty which was a constant 24-hour transmission service ... in the main wireless office ... It was very cramped in there, there was perhaps ... four or five receivers on one bench, and in the middle was where you pass all the signals to and all the bench crowd, they sorted out who was this for and who was that for and [wrote] it all down. You had to write it in your log as you received it ... the messages were all numbered, starting at midnight 00:01 ... and you made sure you got all the numbers down in your log ... as they were transmitted.

Len Beardsley

Beardsley also had to note down the time of origin, date and the name of the addressee of every signal he received. One might imagine that he would thus be better informed than most about what exactly was in store for *Belfast*, but in reality everything was in code and the 18-year-old from Maltby in South Yorkshire was no better informed than anybody else:

> We sat there in Scapa Flow and got ourselves prepared, we didn't know it was D-Day. All we did was revittle the ship, and re-oil and this sort of thing, which were natural, normal things that happened. Of course they were preparing to go down to Normandy but I knew nothing about that nor did any of us. It was only the captain who would know what was going on. So we just got on ... and did our job sort of thing.

The refit provided Captain Parham and his Executive Officer, Commander Philip Welby-Everard, with a chance to overhaul the ship's company as well as her equipment – an opportunity, as Shrimpton remembered, to 'get rid of the square pegs in round holes'. There then followed a brief, intensive period of training and practice, 'working up' to peak efficiency in the bleak waters north of Scotland, where the new members of the crew learned to work with the old, hopefully blending seamlessly into a well-oiled human machine. Bob Shrimpton remembered the process vividly:

You've obviously got new crew members aboard and ... new officers. That's how you find out how the crew is going to knit together with some new officers, some newly made-up petty officers. That working-up period is pretty intense. You're on the go all the time, you go out on gunnery shoots, gunnery practice ... You had one or two members of your mess deck were new so you had to get to know them and to get their characters in with yours, whether you blend together, whether you rely on one another ... And of course you're eyeing up the officers, you go up on the bridge and you see a new officer and you think 'I wonder what he's going to be like!' ... you had to assess things very quickly.

The intensity was of course heightened because, unbeknown to most of those on board, 'the politicians and the generals had planned this D-Day expedition'. For Shrimpton and his comrades it was only with hindsight that 'the little memories slotted together and you realise what was going on'. At the time, most of the men undoubtedly saw it as just more unnecessary hard work for the sake of it – in short, more of what they termed 'Navy Bull'. Ron Jesse realised with hindsight that much of this 'bull' had been deadly serious preparation for the very different kind of war *Belfast* might expect to have to fight off the beaches of Normandy. Rather than a long-range gun battle against the likes of *Scharnhorst* or *Tirpitz*, it would be brief, breathless skirmishing with enemy light coastal craft:

We practiced like crazy for all the sorts of things that might befall us when we were doing bombardments for the Second Front ... We expected to be attacked by submarines and we expected to be attacked by light craft like torpedo boats and so our light guns, our 4-inch guns, were given exhaustive practice in shooting at moving targets. They were primarily for anti-aircraft use, but they could also be depressed for surface firing and they were trained exhaustively to repel torpedo boats. And we uprated our gunnery procedures for bombardment use instead of anti-ship use.

For Jesse, in the engine room, working-up drills mainly consisted of carrying out normal routine but in darkness or by torchlight to simulate the effects of serious damage to the ship. He also vividly recalled the discomfort of training in anti-flash gear, comprising a cloth hood and elbow-length gauntlets to provide some limited protection against the terrible effects of the flash which accompanied an enemy shell hit, which 'could take your skin off'. Wartime anti-flash gear was manufactured from

Above: 'I couldn't make out where it's all been hidden. Why didn't anybody notice these sort of things? ... Where did they come from and how long had they hidden them there!?'– Bob Shrimpton.

British civilians hang out washing and tend their garden in Hill Road, Southampton, phlegmatically ignoring the assembled hardware of an American field howitzer unit parked in Rockleigh Road behind them, waiting for orders to move to the docks and embark for Normandy.

a substance which today we know to be a potentially deadly threat rather than a life-saver – asbestos. At times the men were also expected to train wearing gas masks, a practice which Jesse considered singularly pointless: 'Heaven knows why we were made to carry gas masks around the whole time, the chances of us having to endure a gas attack were vanishingly remote I should have thought, but nevertheless we did.' In fact, for most sailors, the only advantage in carrying a gas mask around all day was the little canvas satchel which held it, an ideal container for those items which were really seen as essential supplies for any enterprising young man who knew he was about to spend 24 hours or longer at actions stations: 'You had a packet of biscuits if you had any sense, you had a little bottle of rum if you had any sense, and you had your cigarettes and a waterproof cigarette lighter. This you always kept by you and you always had it with you when you went to action stations.'

Lieutenant Charles Simpson, Ron Jesse's superior and the man with overall responsibility for the steel-and-copper cathedral in which the Coppersmith worked, would probably have found his youthful flippancy irresponsible. For Simpson, the task in hand as *Belfast* prepared for her greatest challenge was simple, easily stated and vital: 'to ensure that every single item for which we were responsible, whether it was something you could hold in your hand or whether it was the main engine, to make sure that it was up to its highest performance.'

Captain Frederick Parham was of course rather better informed, although he was still not privy to the full information. After Rosyth, the ship returned to Scapa Flow, where his new 'boss' arrived: '... shortly after we got to Scapa my Admiral Robert Burnett was relieved by Vice-Admiral Frederick Dalrymple-Hamilton ... very shortly we were busy preparing for the invasion of Normandy in which we were to lead one of the bombarding squadrons in.' But before the ship left, there was one last important duty at the Royal Navy's windswept, lonely wartime base. For Parham it was a privilege, but also a worrying responsibility: 'Shortly before we left Scapa the fleet was visited by His Majesty the King. And he embarked in the *Belfast* and I took him all round the fleet and eventually back to the mainland.'

Of course, for the rest of the ship's company, a Royal visit simply meant more work. 20-year-old Signalman Lance Tyler recalled one typical piece of service flummery which accompanied King George VI's arrival:

Left: 'Shortly before we left Scapa the fleet was visited by His Majesty the King. And he embarked in the *Belfast* and I took him all round the fleet' — Captain Frederick Parham. The assembled ship's company of HMS *Belfast* cheer the Royal Barge as King George VI departs the ship, May 1944. Having the sovereign aboard was a great compliment to *Belfast*, but a huge amount of extra work for her crew. Many must have breathed a sigh of relief when he finally left.

King George VI came up to visit Scapa and he ... inspected the ship's company. I shall never forget ... we were given three days' notice, and he had to go from the Admiral's bridge down to the Admiral's day cabin for a meal, lunchtime. And the only way they could do it was to have every spare hand painting all the corridors and gangways right down so he would have a nice looking place to go to.

Unfortunately, the task was only partially completed:

For some unknown reason they forgot to paint the handrails on the gangway which went down from the starboard side of the Flag Deck to the Flight Deck ... and the last thing they did before he came on board was to paint this handrail. And so in consequence he, plus I think ... the Admiral, went across the flight deck with a couple of handfuls of aluminium paint all over them.

King George VI returned to the mainland aboard *Belfast* with an escort of nine destroyers, the only occasion in Lance Tyler's naval career that he personally handed a Royal Standard: 'I literally pulled it up as he came on board.' For Parham the visit was a clear success, and the King responded to the ship's hospitality with understated generosity. As he was waiting to be transferred ashore, he sent for Parham in the Admiral's Day Cabin which had formed the temporary Royal quarters. Here, as the Captain remembered: 'really quite shyly, he was sort of fumbling about in his breast pocket and eventually he produced a signed photograph of himself saying "I wondered whether you would like this?"'

For all the unwanted 'spit and polish' the Royal visit had entailed, it was an experience which many of the ship's company would never forget, but almost immediately afterwards it was back to the grim business of war. On 30 May *Belfast* was ordered south from Scapa Flow to the River Clyde where it became suddenly and dramatically obvious to all aboard that whatever the ship was destined for, it was not a return to the dreary, deadly routine of the Arctic Convoys. Bob Shrimpton recalled: 'We saw all these landing craft everywhere [and] we all said "what are those?" cos we'd never seen one before ... The Petty Officer said "they look like landing craft to me" and [we said] "Where are they going?"... "Wouldn't know, probably Italy or something."'

It was somewhere around this time that Lieutenant Andy Palmer was of necessity inducted into Captain Parham's inner circle. Like Commander

William Donald of the *Ulster*, Parham had been issued with Admiral Ramsay's 700-page operational orders, but with the wisdom born of years of experience he immediately decided to delegate the laborious task of wading through them to one or two of his trusted junior officers. Palmer recalled:

> Shortly before the actual event we were issued with a huge volume of the orders for it, and one of the Lieutenants who was a lawyer, Lieutenant B ... and I were ordered to go and segregate ourselves in a cabin and read these very very secret orders in order to brief the admiral and the captain on what the *Belfast* had to do ... We then moved down to the Tail o' the Bank on the Clyde and there we were rearmed and reprovisioned.

The sheer scale of the reprovisioning was a telling indicator to the more perceptive members of the ship's company that a 'big show' might be in the offing. Bob Shrimpton was one of them, noticing with interest that *Belfast* was 'taking on large amounts of ammunition, large amounts of fuel, large amounts of stores, large amounts of medical supplies ...'

While anchored on the Clyde, Admiral Dalrymple-Hamilton took the opportunity to meet the commanding officers of some of the warships anchored around *Belfast*, many of which were small ships with little scope for entertaining. He invited a group of them on board *Belfast* for dinner, including *Ulster*'s Commander William Donald, who remembered the occasion well:

> It was a very memorable evening. The Admiral had a fine presence and inspired us all with his cheerful confidence. With a dozen or more of us around his table, we discussed every topic under the sun from China to Peru. But with all his hospitality and the light-hearted badinage that accompanied it, there was a definite pulse-quickening atmosphere of the 'eve of the battle'.

Neither Parham nor Dalrymple-Hamilton were aware that hundreds of miles to the south, a Very Important Person

Below: 'The Admiral had a fine presence and inspired us all with his cheerful confidence.' – Commander William Donald, HMS *Ulster*.
Rear Admiral Frederick Dalrymple-Hamilton on the bridge of HMS *Belfast*, June 1944. After the war he was appointed Flag Officer, Scotland and Northern Ireland (1946–48) and then Admiral at the British Joint Services Mission in Washington DC (1948–50). Captain Parham is on his right.

was applying the full weight of his not inconsiderable talent for persuasion and bullying to obtaining a ringside seat at the opening of the Second Front. Winston Churchill had summoned the Royal Navy's political head, First Lord of the Admiralty A V Alexander, and its operational chief, the First Sea Lord, Admiral of the Fleet Sir Andrew Cunningham, to inform them both that he intended to go to sea in HMS *Belfast* to watch the invasion. He had, he claimed, already confirmed the arrangement with Admiral Ramsay and Dalrymple-Hamilton himself. Alexander was an astute politician, and 'ABC' was a legendary fighting admiral who had made his name and reputation leading the Mediterranean Fleet to a string of victories, but neither proved able to stand against Churchill in full flow. The situation was only defused by King George VI, who perhaps remembered Parham's courtesy at Scapa Flow and, as a former naval officer himself, probably realised just how inconvenient and dangerous it would be for *Belfast* to carry such a person on the first, riskiest day of the operation. The King stated that if Churchill was to go, then he would have to go himself as the head of all three armed services. Churchill reluctantly conceded, and there the matter ended.

All over the ship, more and more men were starting to be given snippets of information; clues which when taken together made her final role, if not her final destination, steadily more obvious. Peter Brooke Smith was a Lieutenant in the Royal Naval Volunteer Reserve, a pre-war schoolteacher who now found himself in command of one of *Belfast's* 4-inch secondary armament Directors. His diary and unpublished memoir provide an articulate and dramatic account of the events of June 1944 (see Primary Sources, IWM Department of Documents). As *Belfast* swung sedately at anchor on the Clyde, he noted another tell-tale sign: 'We landed our spare boats (Admiral's barge, 3rd motor boat and pinnace) to save top weight and lessen fire risk.' Brooke Smith also managed to get ashore, where much to his friends' amusement he took the opportunity to obtain what he doubtless saw as essential campaign supplies: 'I picked up Smetana's *Moldau* and Beethoven's *Fifth*, though some of my friends thought it foolish to buy records at that time considering the chance of losing them during the coming events.'

Charles Bunbury was one of *Belfast's* Midshipmen in June 1944, essentially a junior officer who was completing the final element of his instruction at sea. As part of his training, he had to keep a detailed journal. Now in the IWM Department of Documents (see Primary Sources), it provides a marvellous record of the Normandy fighting. On 2 June he attended a lecture given by the ship's Gunnery Officer, Lieutenant-Commander Rex Mountifield, who gave a clear taste of the overwhelming air superiority which the Allies were to enjoy over Normandy. Friendly fire – that wonderful military euphemism – was to be the biggest worry as far as anti-aircraft gunners were concerned:

> He discussed chiefly the rules laid down for determining whether an aircraft is friendly or hostile during an attack on the enemy coast. All British fighter aircraft were to be painted with black and white stripes on the underside of the wings and fuselage. An aircraft is to be considered hostile if it is definitely diving on or attacking the ship, but friendly if it gives correct signals, complies with radar, has its undercarriage down, is towing a glider, is four-engined or a biplane.

According to *Belfast*'s log, while Charles Bunbury attended his lecture the ship was being held on two hours' notice for steam (Log 1). Ominously, earlier in the evening five cruisers and the veteran battleships *Warspite* and *Ramilles* weighed anchor and slipped away. All these ships were destined to form part of the Eastern Naval Task Force. Ron Jesse remembered an atmosphere of 'high excitement', the battleships proceeding majestically down the Clyde 'with all flags flying and the band playing'. Then it was *Belfast*'s turn. At 11:00 hours on 3 June, the cruiser weighed anchor. After a brief practice shoot with her 4-inch secondary armament, she began the long journey south, down through the Irish Sea to the Channel. Charles Bunbury recorded that, 'there was a thick mist and heavy drizzle, but in spite of that our band was playing on the quarterdeck'. By this stage, although no formal announcement had been made, *Belfast*'s job was no longer a secret. According to Ron Jesse: 'Everybody knew what we were off to do, nobody knew where or when but everybody knew what we were off to do and it was an atmosphere of high excitement and we could almost see the end of the war just over the horizon. Of course that was not to be but nevertheless that was the atmosphere and we sailed off under darkened ship ... down the Irish Sea.'

It is not hard to imagine the sense of growing anticipation, as *Belfast* and her consorts steamed steadily south through the Irish Sea, watching the armada steadily increase in size as ships and boats of all descriptions emerged from remote Scottish ports and anchorages to 'button on' to the various convoys. With hindsight it was a time of high drama, but for many of the men, like Len Beardsley, it was simply 'business as usual':

We set sail and came down through the Scottish Islands and picked up landing craft and victualling ships and such like, and there was a great big convoy all sailed down past Wales and past Cornwall and down into the channel ... I was so damned busy I hadn't got time to think ... Off duty, I never gave it much thought, just got on with the job, here I am I'm on this ship and I might as well make the most of it and 'sing a happy song' sort of thing. What's the use of complaining? It ain't going to do you any good so I just got on with it!

As the ship steamed south through the Irish Sea to the English Channel, those men who had the time to watch observed, according to Bunbury's journal, 'literally thousands of ships' heading the same way. Peter Brooke Smith noted 'a slow convoy of incredibly ancient-looking merchant ships, including also the Dutch cruiser *Sumatra*'. Much later he realised that these superannuated ships were the Corncobs, destined to be scuttled as breakwaters as part of the Mulberry harbour.

Miraculously, the gigantic operation seemed to be proceeding entirely according to plan, until nature dramatically intervened. The exact date and time of the landings had been dependant on a complex set of environmental conditions. In particular a full or near-full moon was absolutely vital, as it would provide illumination for aircraft pilots and have the highest tides. The Allies wanted to land just before dawn, midway between low and high tide, with the tide coming in. This would improve the visibility of obstacles on the beach, while minimising the amount of time the men had to spend exposed in the open. With these conditions in mind, Eisenhower had chosen 5 June for the assault. On the 4 June it became miserably clear that the weather the next day was going to be wholly unsuitable. A gale had blown up, and the high winds and heavy seas would make it impossible to launch landing craft. Furthermore, low cloud cover meant that the Allies' overwhelming air superiority, the invasion's greatest advantage, would be gravely compromised, and landing paratroops on the correct drop zones would be extremely difficult and dangerous.

Eisenhower's 'weather man' was an RAF meteorological officer named Group Captain James Stagg. On the evening of 4 June he met the general, and convinced him that the weather would improve sufficiently for the invasion to proceed on 6 June. It is almost impossible to imagine the weight of responsibility Eisenhower felt as he made this critical decision. Historian Max Hastings has written that 'at no single period did the Supreme Commander distinguish himself more than by his judgement and

decision during the D-Day launching conferences of 3–4 June'. Brushing aside objections by Leigh-Mallory and Tedder, he courageously pushed the button for 6 June: 'I'm quite positive we must give the order. I don't like it but there it is ... I don't see how we can possibly do anything else'.

D-Day was on. Had Eisenhower deferred to his senior commanders, the next available date would have been between 18 and 20 June, when as it turned out, the weather was even worse. His adversaries' weather intelligence was nowhere near as comprehensive, as the Kriegsmarine's weather-reporting ships had been largely driven from the Atlantic, forcing the Germans to rely on sporadic and often inaccurate reports from busy,

Above: 'Literally thousands of ships' – Charles Bunbury. Landing craft at the quayside in Southampton, 1944. Most are LCTs, but a pair of Landing Craft (Headquarters) can be seen in the centre. LCH were Infantry Landing Craft, fitted with radar and communications equipment to convert them into a headquarters ship for a group of assault craft.

distracted U-boat commanders. Consequently, they anticipated two weeks of unbroken foul weather. Commanders left their posts to attend war games in Rennes, and many men were given leave. Field Marshal Erwin Rommel, once again Montgomery's chief opponent, returned to Germany for his wife's birthday and to meet with Hitler.

Of course, nobody on *Belfast* was privy to this information. For them the weather delay, one of D-Day's most dramatic moments, simply meant an entirely incomprehensible decision to steam in circles in appalling weather for a night, a process which even the usually phlegmatic Captain Parham described as 'a little trying for the nerves'. Decades later, many of them could not even recall precisely where they were, although most seem to agree it was somewhere around Lundy Island in the Bristol Channel. Ron Jesse recalled:

Above: In an unidentified British port, heavily laden, grim-faced US assault troops file aboard a tiny, uncomfortable LCA (Landing Craft Assault) before the invasion. Each man was carrying on average 75 pounds (34 kg) of equipment when he stepped on to the Normandy beaches. By 6 June 1944, there were over 1.5 million American soldiers, sailors and airmen in the UK.

When we got to the north coast of Cornwall the project was put back 24 hours, so we had to waste 24 hours ... We sailed round and round Lundy Island I remember, and first of all we went twice round one way and then turned round and went twice round the other way because we were getting giddy, but we just had to lose time before we picked up the schedule.

Charles Bunbury noted in his journal that: 'When I went on watch at 08:00 there was a strong wind and a heavy swell, which was the last thing I expected, and certainly not what we wanted for the invasion. The barometer was falling quite fast and it looked as if it would get worse.'

At least the crews of the warships could ride out the storm in relative comfort. Conditions were appalling for the assault troops, many of whom were already at sea, crammed into their landing craft. Peter Brooke Smith wrote how: 'We overhauled convoy after convoy of landing craft of all descriptions, loaded with vehicles and crammed with British and American soldiers. We pitied them in those small ships without much shelter from the choppy sea. They must have spent two or three days in extremely cramped confinement waiting for the signal to sail.' Leslie Coleman also saw the hapless soldiers in their landing craft, and Captain Parham's characteristically compassionate response to their plight: 'they'd been stuck there from the day before ... and we steamed as close as we could to them to morale boost them, and they went mad, cheering and everything else ... imagine if you were in the middle of the sea and nobody with you at all and then we see them there.' Bob Shrimpton remembered Parham going even further to alleviate conditions for the hapless assault troops.

Above: 'We overhauled convoy after convoy of landing craft of all descriptions, loaded with vehicles and crammed with British and American soldiers.' – Peter Brooke Smith. Oil painting by war artist Stephen Bone, showing LCTs and Landing Craft Mechanised (LCM) heading to France beneath their protective umbrella of barrage balloons. Bone was the son of Sir Muirhead Bone, who was a noted war artist during the First World War.

Those army lads sitting in those landing craft, they were having a hell of a time, so ... the skipper made the ship circle around this block of landing craft and I think ... he sprayed some oil on the water and that had a tendency to drop the waves down so it only became a swell. It broke up the choppy waves and it helped to relieve the tension aboard those landing craft ... It's a wonder we were never spotted...

Charles Bunbury remembered the very real risk of catastrophe for men trapped in craft which were simply not designed to cope with heavy weather: 'In the afternoon we passed several large convoys of LSTs, LCTs and Rhinos [a type of ferry] ... they [the Rhinos] ... looked just like rafts made up of many watertight compartments like petrol tins ... they all carried vehicles and men and some had tents pitched on them. They must have been extremely uncomfortable, knowing that at any time ... they might capsize.' Conditions on the flat-bottomed landing craft were indeed appalling. 19-year-old Private Leslie Perry of the Suffolk Regiment was on one:

The landing craft started to toss and turn. Being flat-bottomed they were just bobbing about like corks. That is when I started being sick. The officer was the first one to the rail, and I followed him, and I was sick all the way over. I was sitting on top of the stairs munching biscuits and sipping water because when you're retching and you haven't got anything to eat it just tears you to pieces.

Above: They looked just like rafts ... they all carried vehicles and men, and some had tents pitched on them. They must have been extremely uncomfortable, knowing that at any time they might capsize.' – Charles Bunbury. Doubtful American sailors watch through the bow doors of a Tank Landing Ship as a crowded Rhino Ferry slowly heads for the beaches near Isigny. Rhinos were crude flat-bottomed barges made from several connected pontoons powered by outboard engines. They could also be filled with water and used as piers.

Finally, Parham and Dalrymple-Hamilton received the signal they had been waiting for. Stagg had convinced Eisenhower that better weather was on its way, and the invasion was on for 6 June. *Belfast* turned south for the last time, and the two officers determined that the time was right to tell the ship's company what many of them almost certainly already knew. 'That was the only occasion during the two years I was in command that I addressed the ship's company over the loudspeaker', Parham remembered years later, revealing the empathy which many of those under his command felt characterised his leadership style. 'I always said that when I talk to my men I like to see them. Of course in this case it was impossible and I spoke to them over the loudspeaker and told them exactly what we were going to do.' Most of *Belfast*'s crew recalled the announcement, although for some it meant more than for others. Larry Fursland was one of the less sentimental: 'Eventually they told us over the SRE system, the tannoy system … they told us that that we were going to do [the] landings at Normandy.' Brian Butler remembered that 'we were pleased, we were glad we were getting on with the invasion because there'd been talk about it for such a long time and we were glad that it was eventually going to happen'.

Bob Shrimpton, typically, remembered the humorous side of this historic announcement:

> The weather lifted and I vividly remember the tannoy. We were sitting in the mess deck and the tannoy came on and it was the Captain speaking and he said 'we are now going to embark on the invasion of the beaches at Normandy'. And there was dead silence and then the padre came on and he said a few words and had a prayer and it switched itself off and everybody thought 'well this is it'. And then this old Leading Seaman in the opposite mess, he said 'well it's about time we had a cup of tea then, looks like we might not get another one'. And that was when we first heard about the landing at Normandy.

Lieutenant-Commander Charles Simpson was rather more thoughtful, aware not only of the importance of the task which lay ahead of them but perhaps also of the dangers inherent in taking part in the greatest seaborne invasion in history. 'We were summoned to listen to the ship's broadcast', he remembered years afterwards, 'This was an order not a request, and all because the admiral was going to address us over the loudspeaker'. The men gathered in silence around the nearest loudspeaker, all over the ship, in passageways and mess decks, workshops, shell rooms and magazines, from the lofty heights of the bridge superstructure to engine and boiler rooms, buried deep down inside *Belfast*'s steel hull. 'So on came the admiral's voice and he announced that we had left harbour to take part in the biggest military encounter the world will have ever known. We were, when weather conditions permitted, to take part in the invasion of France.'

Simpson remembered:

> ... great excitement, subdued jubilation. It was going to be a day that was going to remain in history. One appreciated that from the moment the admiral started talking. He had said this is the greatest invasion the world had ever seen ... this was his prognosis. So, subdued excitement. One knew there were perils to be met under conditions we had never before had thought about ... I waited to see what was going to happen.

Peter Brooke Smith summarised Dalrymple-Hamilton's words in his diary. From it we learn that the Admiral was not perhaps as matter-of-fact as some of the men under his command remembered. According to Brooke Smith, Dalrymple-Hamilton quoted extensively from the Bible, specifically the Book of Job, Chapter 3, Verse 13:

> Put ye in the sickle, for the harvest is ripe: come get you down, for the press is full, the fats overflow; for their wickedness is great. Multitudes, multitudes in the valley of decision: for the day of the Lord is near in the valley of decision. The sun and the moon shall be darkened, and the stars shall withdraw their shining. The Lord also shall roar out of Zion, and utter his voice from Jerusalem; and the heavens and the earth shall shake: but the Lord will be the hope of his people, and the strength of the children of Israel. So shall ye know that I am the Lord your God dwelling in Zion, my holy mountain: then shall Jerusalem be holy, and there shall no stranger pass through her anymore.

Perhaps suddenly and painfully aware that these sombre lines might not be seen as entirely encouraging by everyone aboard, Dalrymple-Hamilton then changed tack, choosing, like many a commander before him on the eve of battle, to take heart from the words of Shakespeare's Henry V:

> And gentlemen of England now a-bed,
> Shall think themselves accursed they were not here,
> And hold their manhoods cheap whilst any speaks,
> That fought with us upon St Crispin's Day.

As *Belfast* forged her way through the darkness and gradually lessening seas, rounding Land's End into the Channel, Captain Parham ordered his men to second-degree readiness, one stage short of 'action stations'. Calmly, quietly, their efficient, economical movements doubtless masking a multitude of emotions, nearly a thousand mostly very young men trudged through narrow steel passageways or hauled themselves up and down ladders until they reached the mostly cramped and uncomfortable spaces in which they would spent the next few days. For Peter Brooke Smith this meant 'a most uncomfortable 3½ hours cat-napping under my director on the hangar top'.

Wireless Operator Len Beardsley remembered the Admiral's speech as something of a starting gun: 'all of a sudden "go"' and that was it, off we all went charging down to Normandy. I didn't know where the hell we were going!' As *Belfast* entered the Channel, more and more ships and craft came into sight, ploughing through the choppy seas in the darkness, filled with the pale, anxious faces of the assault troops, most of them no older than *Belfast*'s crew – teenagers and young men in their early 20s – who given the choice would doubtless have preferred to be chasing girls around their home towns rather than chasing Germans out of occupied France. Trooper Ronald Mole of the 4th/7th Royal Dragoon Guards described himself as 'innocent as a new-born babe ... never had any experiences before'.

Those of *Belfast*'s crew who were fortunate enough to be on the upper deck and able to see were staggered at the scale of the invasion fleet. 'All these barges full of soldiers and supply ships and that sort of thing and the other warships that were with us at the time', recalled Len Beardsley, before continuing with pardonable exaggeration: 'Zillions of ships everywhere, it was unbelievable, there wasn't barely room to sail anywhere. You'd bump into everything or everybody unless you were careful. They did very well considering.' The young Coppersmith Ron Jesse was also on deck, near his cramped little workshop beneath the funnel, from where he was able to wave to the sea-sick soldiers, and cheer them. Interviewed in 2003 he was still visibly moved by the experience, pausing from time to time to choke back tears:

We were at cruising stations ... and waved and cheered to all the soldiers ... the soldiers in their landing craft were all waving back and full of tearfulness and we were overhauling dozens of them as we went along the south coast. They were all coming out of their little harbours before taking up their allotted stations and then that night we turned south as we passed the Isle of Wight and made our way slowly across the English Channel according to the schedule so as to arrive off the French Coast at six the next morning.

Jesse was particularly struck by the tank landing craft, ugly steel shoeboxes wallowing along at a steady 8 knots, or 15 km/h, in lines of 6:

We would overhaul one line of 6 and everybody was waving and cheering and then we'd go on a bit further and there was another line of 6 and I suppose we must have passed something like 50 of them going through quite a choppy sea. They were on their decks and the tanks were down inside, they were tank landing craft mainly, and so we turned south off The Needles and spent the night going down across the channel behind the minesweepers so as to arrive off the beaches at six o'clock.

As *Belfast* neared the great naval base at Portsmouth, the invasion fleet increased in size until the amazed sailors found themselves staring out at an armada of almost inconceivable vastness. Many struggled for appropriate words to describe it. Joseph Stagno was just 17, a Gibraltarian who had been evacuated to first Morocco and then to Scotland on the outbreak of war. He had joined *Belfast* at the end of 1943, and was understandably awed by the sight of the invasion fleet: 'If you looked across from the Isle of Wight you could have walked across to France on ships and landing craft!' For Lance Tyler it was quite simply 'a fantastic sight that I shall never ever see again'. Larry Fursland was another man who could barely tear himself away from the extraordinary sight, even when he went off watch in the middle of the night. After a quick shower, he snuck up to a perfect vantage point he had already identified, on the well deck by the redundant aircraft catapult, from where he could watch history being made:

I never went down below, I enjoyed every [chance] to see what's happening. Once we got round Lands End I've never seen such an armada in all my life! All the bays and all the coast, ships of every description coming out. Eventually we went up through the coast, Portsmouth, and all those ships coming out, hundreds of them, hundreds ... I'd never forget it.

Lieutenant Andy Palmer was passing time on the bridge, staring out into the darkness at the passing assault craft. Although the storm had abated the conditions were still dreadful, and he was overwhelmed by

Above: 'We would overhaul one line of 6 and everybody was waving and cheering
and then we'd go on a bit further and there was another line of 6 and I suppose we must
have passed something like 50 of them going through quite a choppy sea' — Ron Jesse.
In rough seas and under a gloomy sky, a convoy of LCTs and supply ships depart Spithead
for Normandy.

sympathy for the hapless soldiers. Like many sailors, he much preferred his own wartime life, hard though it might be, to that of a 'pongo':

> I can remember leaning over the side of the bridge in the dark and saying 'you poor buggers'. It was windy, it was the aftermath of a gale so it was fairly rough, many of them were seasick, most of them must have been cold and wet and when they got to the other end they were going to be asked to assault prepared defences on the beaches. I wouldn't be a soldier.

By now, Captain Parham was far too preoccupied with the navigational challenge posed by hundreds of tiny invasion craft to spare much thought to the plight of the occupants:

> There was a very strong cross-tide running and we had, by the programme which had been worked out in the minutest detail, to have during this time overtaken millions of landing craft full of soldiers. Thank heaven there was a full moon, because I think we were almost continuously ... dodging these landing craft, and if there hadn't been a full moon I dread to think how many of them we would have sunk.

The invasion had reached the point of no return. From all along the south coast of England, squadrons and flotillas were emerging – first the Americans of Force U from Brixham, Dartmouth and Salcombe, and Force O from Weymouth, Poole and Portland; then the British of Forces G, J and S, mostly from the Solent and the great south coast ports of Southampton and Portsmouth, but some units from as far east as Shoreham. The thousands of ships, large and small, converged on a focal point some 20 miles south of Hayling Island. This was Assembly Area Z, informally known as 'Piccadilly Circus', which was marked by a large blue-and-white striped 'Z Buoy' fitted with a bell and a flashing light. From 'Piccadilly Circus' stretched a fan of five lines of marker buoys, each with a light shining back towards the English coast. 30 miles from Normandy, the single lines became five double lines with a swept channel in between, each pointing at one of the invasion beaches.

Through this carefully prepared maritime highway, the ships of the invasion fleet steamed south to their assigned stations off the Normandy coast. In the lead were the minesweepers, understated and largely unsung heroes of Operation 'Neptune', whose terrifying responsibility was to covertly sweep ten safe channels through both the British and German minefields which barred the way to Normandy. Collectively, these ten channels became known as 'The Spout', through which the invasion fleet would pour. 'Our minesweepers', wrote Peter Brooke Smith, 'did a magnificent job, sweeping right up to the invasion beaches, under the nose of the enemy, without interference'. Behind them crept landing craft, large and small, wallowing landing ships, headquarters ships, destroyers, cruisers, battleships, supply ships, Corncobs, motor torpedo boats, barges, lighters, rescue launches and the countless other craft which made up Operation 'Neptune'.

Right in the lead, immediately behind the minesweepers heading into Juno beach, was HMS *Belfast*. Perhaps predictably, of all the ship's company it is *Belfast*'s quietly spoken Senior Engineer, Charles Simpson, who has left the most eloquent, dignified account of that long, silent journey through the darkness to the Normandy beaches:

> It was exceptionally quiet almost to the point of being ghostly. We joined the armada that assembled off the coast of Cornwall and Devon to proceed up the English Channel and it was all done in intense silence ... We were at a subdued state of readiness until we arrived off what proved to be the invasion coast, so although we were approaching the scene of invasion it was still sufficiently far away for us not to be at an advanced state of readiness which enabled us to go on the upper deck. The armada stretched for miles and miles and miles so we were able to see what became the

Left: Serious faced men of 4 Commando, 1st Special Service Brigade, receive a last-minute briefing from their commanding officer, Lieutenant-Colonel Robert Dawson, before D-Day. Two troops of 4 Commando were formed from Free French soldiers. They landed at Ouistreham on 6 June, possibly supported at some point by fire from HMS *Belfast*. Dawson was wounded on 6 June, but returned to resume command and survived the war.

beginning of the invasion for us ... Miles and miles of small craft carrying soldiers. They sat or stood in the open air in utter silence and when we had proceeded up these lines sufficiently long, you could turn and look astern and see these lines disappearing over the horizon it was so long. Then when the captain or admiral deemed it proper we were sent to our action stations and I imagine that for the last 40 miles of approach in no time we got to D-Day landing, our particular part of France which we were to engage in gunfire.

Charles Bunbury wrote in his journal of the difficulty of navigating in such narrow waters: 'We were going very slowly and keeping between lines of lighted buoys which we always had to find ... which had been dropped by minesweepers which were far ahead of us. We overtook masses of landing craft of all varieties that were all heading the same way and they were very hard to see in the darkness.'

As dusk fell Admiral Dalrymple-Hamilton sent a signal to the ships under his command, turning from Shakespeare and the Bible to cricket for his final words: 'Best of luck to you all. Keep a good length and your eye on the middle stump, and we shall soon have the enemy all out'. *Belfast* had arrived, and her 'longest day' was about to begin.

Above: The brooding calm before the storm. A dramatic oil painting by war artist Robert Eurich, showing tanks lining up to board an LST through its yawning bow doors. Behind, the sea is covered with every conceivable type of invasion craft, including landing craft, destroyers, a Rhino ferry and a tug towing sections of Mulberry harbour. Eurich was a marine artist from Southampton, and probably painted the scene from his own observations.

CHAPTER FOUR
THE LONGEST DAY

'Soldiers, Sailors and Airmen of the Allied Expeditionary
Forces! You are about to embark upon the Great Crusade,
towards which we have striven these many months.
The eyes of the world are upon you.'
General Eisenhower's Order of the Day, 6 June 1944

In the early hours of the morning *Belfast* went to action stations. Peter Brooke Smith recorded the moment: 'At 4am we went to action stations, and already could see the glow of red fires being started by our bombers, and the streams of red tracers being sent up by the enemy's ack-ack [anti-aircraft fire]. As it grew lighter we began to make out the coastline, fairly low-lying in our sector, but with steep cliffs to the westward.' The planning for Operation 'Neptune' had been meticulous. Like every other ship in the bombardment forces, *Belfast* had an allocated spot, some five or six miles offshore, off the small resorts towns of Ver-sur-Mer and Ouistreham, marked by a Dan Buoy, a marker buoy with coded flag on top. At 05:00, Captain Parham brought his ship into position, and dropped anchor. *Belfast* was ready.

George Burridge's action station on 6 June 1944 was in the Radar Plot Room, responsible for trying to make sense of the mass of shipping and aircraft which surrounded *Belfast*. For him, D-Day was a major professional headache: 'The whole sea was full of ships and landing craft and we were surrounded by all sorts of ships ... I was still in the plot, that was still my action station, and ... it was almost a hopeless position ... from a plotting point of view because there were so many ships there.' Bewildered and bombarded with information, Burridge and his colleagues essentially gave up, remembering that 'we knew they were all our ships anyway, so we were less active than in previous situations'.

Many *Belfast* veterans, like Lance Tyler, believe that their ship was the first to open fire on 6 June 1944: '... we literally opened up the very first salvo on HMS *Belfast* at about twenty past five in the morning and I've never ever seen so many ships, landing craft, corvettes, frigates you name it, and I don't suppose anyone will ever see the like of it ever again'. Sadly, however, this does not seem to have been the case, although more by accident than design. The first targets for the bombarding ships were predetermined – coastal batteries and other defence installations which had been carefully identified as part of the painstaking intelligence work which had predated D-Day, and then plotted on charts and maps for issue to each ship as part of their individually tailored 700-page orders. But picking out a concealed target several miles offshore, in the grey hazy dawn light and already starting to be obscured by smoke rising from the intense aerial bombing which had begun earlier, was not easy. Captain Parham and his senior Gunnery Officer, Lieutenant-Commander Rex Mountifield, were struggling to identify the first target, a German battery near the village of La Marefontaine. But if Parham and Mountifield

Left: 'It just was motionless in the water [and] it began firing these rockets. It fired literally hundreds of them, the landing craft was just enveloped in a pall of smoke.' – Brian Butler.
Landing Craft (Rocket) off Juno Area, 6 June 1944. The rockets can be seen in flight above the ship. Designed to saturate the beach before landing, these converted tank landing craft had an additional deck above the tank deck on which rocket launching racks were mounted. 5,000 spare rockets were stored below in the now enclosed tank deck.

Left: Aerial reconnaissance photograph of the formidable German gun battery at Merville, 3 km east of Ouistreham, after aerial bombardment in May 1944. Bombing failed to penetrate the concrete gun positions and, because of the threat the battery posed to the landings on Sword Area, it was attacked and captured by 9th Battalion, The Parachute Regiment, in the early hours of 6 June.

Right: 'We were furiously indignant when at 05:23 a cruiser to the westward of us, probably HMS *Orion*, opened fire and thus forestalled us the honour of being the first ship to fire a shot in the Second Front.' – Peter Brooke Smith. The veteran Mediterranean Fleet cruiser HMS *Orion* fires a broadside off the Normandy beaches, with HMS *Belfast* dimly visible in the background.

made the wrong call and the four ex-Czech 100mm howitzers from *Artillerie-Regiment 1716* were left unmolested, they could cause untold harm to the vulnerable assault troops. The consequences could be disastrous, and the two senior officers knew perfectly well that a few moments spent carefully checking were well worth it. For Brooke Smith and the younger officers and men, though, anxious to get moving, it was intensely frustrating: 'All positions were seething with impatience! "What the hell's the delay? Let's get cracking for god's sake!!"'

Andy Palmer was another junior officer who could not understand the delay: 'I stood on the bridge and I thought "it's getting daylight why don't we do something!?" He later came to understand that the planning for 'Neptune' had been meticulous, conceding that his superiors had known exactly what was going on and understood the vital importance of everybody identifying their correct target:

> The whole ... operation ... was planned in a very detailed way. Admiral Ramsay was a marvellous man. We knew every ship, and there were over a thousand ships involved in this. Everybody knew exactly where to go and anchor, and exactly when to open fire ... The time arrived eventually and

the word went off and the *Belfast* fired. I believe, I really believe, she fired the very first salvo and I smugly stood there on the bridge and I said, 'There you are the first shot in the battle to liberate Europe'.

In fact, while Parham and Mountifield deliberated, the race, if such it was, had been lost. Brooke Smith wrote:

We were furiously indignant when at 05:23 a cruiser to the westward of us, probably HMS *Orion*, opened fire and thus forestalled us the honour of being the first ship to fire a shot in the Second Front. We need not have worried: Rex North, *Sunday Pictorial*'s war correspondent who we had onboard, not only unblushingly gave us that honour, but dramatised a most lurid account of the subsequent proceedings for his readers.

Belfast's log records that she opened fire three minutes later, at 05:27, 'with full broadside to port' (Log 1). Charles Bunbury wrote:

At 05:00 we stopped about five miles off the coast, in a mine swept area, with the *Diadem* near us. The coast was now slowly becoming more plainly visible, and the whole time I expected to see flashes from ashore, the enemy defence batteries firing at us: but nothing fired at us and I couldn't think why ... at 05:27 we started firing at a pre-arranged target, a thick-concrete-encased battery.

Above: 'At 0527 we started firing at a pre-arranged target, a thick-concrete-encased battery.'
– Charles Bunbury.
HMS *Belfast* at anchor off the Normandy beachhead, firing steadily from her two forward turrets, A and B, as she begins to suppress the German gun battery at la Marefontaine.

20-year-old Ordinary Seaman Gordon 'Putty' Painter was a Gun Layer in B Turret, the second of the two forward triple 6-inch turrets. He had no idea what exactly he was firing at. HMS *Belfast* had a centralised fire-control system; what Painter's turret fired at was controlled by the cruiser's Gunnery Officer, up high in the Director Control Tower, where the sighting instruments were located. The process was essentially a triangle. Brooke Smith and his team used the ship's range-finding equipment to measure the elevation and bearing to the target. This information was sent to the Transmitting Station, where another team used a mechanical computer known as an Admiralty Fire Control Table to calculate the angle to which the turrets should be turned and the elevation to which the guns should be raised or lowered. This information was then sent to the turrets, where the gunlayers – like Gordon Painter – adjusted the elevation of their guns to match. A Turret Layer carried out the same process for the bearing (the direction which the turret should face). When the guns were on target, the Captain of the Turret reported it promptly and the guns were centrally fired.

Gordon Painter

The entire process had to be carried out quickly and efficiently, the entire ship operating as a well-drilled machine with every individual playing a small, clearly defined but absolutely vital role. If Painter was too slow in responding to the information, it would be out of date before the guns were fired and the ship would miss her target, a responsibility of which he was only too aware:

> The gunlayer's job and the gun trainer's job are quite important jobs because you govern the movement of the guns themselves. We basically had to follow pointers manually. The instructions would come down from the bridge and their instructions would move a point on my dials which I had to follow and if you don't follow it and you start to fire the guns then you're in trouble because the shells are going to fall short or ... too far right or too far left or whatever. One had to ... be alert and keep up with it ... we had quite a small periscope in the roof of the turret but basically ... that's the only view of the outside that you would have.

Once the ship went to action stations, Painter was locked into his turret, sealed in a steel box, programmed into his monotonous but vital routines like a piece of the ship's equipment and assaulted by constant noise, with little or no awareness of what was going on outside:

It was quite noisy of course! We were firing broadsides, which means that all the guns were firing together – the whole lot. You get ... twelve 6-inch guns firing, it rocks the ship backwards and forward and this continually going on. I think we did have ... something to put in your ears, if you didn't you'd soon go deaf. The only time we could leave [the turret] was if nature called and then you had somebody to take over.

But before he was locked down, he had caught a glimpse of the extraordinary events in which he was about to play a small but vital part. The visual imprint stayed with him for decades:

We were if you like the spearhead, we were very honoured ... I do remember before we were locked in our turrets ... the sky being lit up over France and with the fires started by the Royal Air Force bombing. I also remember seeing hundreds and hundreds of landing craft and small ships all going across. I think I'm right in saying that some of these had barrage balloons up to stop the German aircraft attacking too low. And then ... we started our bombardment about half past five that morning.

Not everyone was as well-prepared for the start of the bombardment. Leslie Coleman was a cordite handler in one of the 6-inch turrets, another monotonous but essential task: 'You have a pedal ... for the cordite to come up and when you push your foot down one comes up in a case.' He was on the upper deck making his way to his action station when the gunfire began; announcements may well have been made but Coleman did not hear them: 'I think about 5 o'clock on D-Day, June the 6th, all of a sudden I was on the upper deck and "crash bang wallop" type of thing! My head was nearly taken off and cordite came into my eyes, because nobody said "right we're going to fire!" You just ... away it went like.'

Belfast's first target, the gun battery at La Marefontaine, was unfinished. It was one of the many extra defence works ordered by Rommel when he was appointed to inspect the German defences of northwest Europe at the end of 1943. It consisted of four casemates (gun positions), rapidly constructed by simply pouring concrete between two parallel stone walls. The battery lacked the network of protective infantry trenches and foxholes which characterised the older defences in Normandy, and the gunners could not look directly onto the beaches to fire at their targets. Instead, much like *Belfast*'s guns, their fire was controlled from a rangefinder at a command post, known as Widerstandnest 32b, hidden on a nearby wooded hill. The various elements of the battery were linked by buried telephone cables. Thanks to *Belfast*'s intense and accurate bombardment, La Marefontaine played no meaningful role in the defence of the beaches. The badly demoralised garrison was subsequently attacked by fighter bombers, encircled, and finally captured by the 7th Battalion, the Green Howards, supported by some of Hobart's 79th Armoured Division 'Funnies' – Churchill Crocodile flamethrowing tanks from 141 Regiment, Royal Armoured Corps. *Belfast*, and her people, had performed their first task admirably.

Denis Watkinson

According to Andy Palmer, Gunnery Officer Rex Mountifield went ashore a few days after the landings, once the area had been secured, to inspect La Marefontaine battery and see what the effect of *Belfast*'s fire had been. Mountifield reported back with chilling matter-of-factness that 'we really mangled that battery'. Perhaps it was Mountifield who posted the note on the ship's notice board remembered by Denis Watkinson, one of *Belfast*'s 4-inch gunners. Although only 18 years old, Watkinson had already lived through the Liverpool Blitz, which perhaps explains his empathy for those on the receiving end of the bombardment: 'They put it on the notice board that we'd destroyed the whole place and ... only [one] German ... came out of it. It wasn't a very nice thing to see, lives being wasted doesn't matter whether you're German or British or what you are it's not nice.' Watkinson was at his action station on the upper deck, with a clear view, and his recollections of that June morning are notably vivid:

> The bombers were bombing and you could see the planes, some of them had been brought down and things like this you know, and eventually as light was breaking we were on our own. Our convoys were well behind of us, the landing craft and the like. And we spread out, the three cruisers spread out along the beaches and it looked ever so peaceful after seeing all the fires and the bombing during the night, it looked so quiet and peaceful, the churches on the hills.

Watkinson remembered the confidence instilled by being in a ship of *Belfast*'s size and power, alongside the greatest armada the world had ever seen:

> You're in a big ship and you're behind a big gun which changes your thinking altogether ... When we opened fire, first thing we heard was 'X and Y turrets will be opening up in five minutes time!'... then they opened fire. Well that's

when things started! They were taken by surprise, there's no two ways about it, and then they started to fire back but they were more concerned about the landing parties, and merchant ships things like that. For all they had a go at us and other ships they were more concerned with stopping the men getting ashore. You could see a lot of people not getting ashore and boats getting hit ... blowing up and flames in the water things like that.

At 06:05 *Belfast*'s log records an alarming moment, when the cruiser HMS *Scylla* reported three enemy destroyers manoeuvring to attack the invasion fleet (Log 1). By June 1944 the Kriegsmarine, always far smaller than the Royal Navy, had almost ceased to exist; in fact Andy Palmer had been removed from his beloved torpedoes to become an air defence controller because, as he succinctly put it, 'clearly there were going to be no torpedo targets because the German Navy's ships which might have intervened effectively had been sunk'. However, that service had certainly not lost its fighting spirit. All that the Germans had available to deploy against the hundreds of battleships, cruisers, destroyers, frigates, sloops and countless smaller craft which had suddenly appeared off the coast were a handful of *schnellbooten*, the fast, well-armed motor torpedo boats known to the Allies as 'E-boats' (for 'enemy boats'), and the small destroyers of 5.Torpedobootsflotille, based at Le Havre.

Although catastrophically outnumbered and utterly incapable of doing any serious harm to the invasion fleet, this tiny force heroically put to sea just before dawn on 6 June. The torpedo boats *Jaguar* and *Moewe* even managed to get within firing range, launching a salvo of torpedoes at the warships off Sword beach, one of which hit the Norwegian destroyer HNoMS *Svenner* amidships. *Svenner* exploded dramatically and broke in two, before sinking in minutes with the loss of 32 Norwegian crew members and one Briton. (*Svenner* was formerly the British destroyer HMS *Shark*.) British Commando Captain Kenneth Wright witnessed her end: 'It was rather appalling. The ship just cracked in half, and the two ends folded together as if it were a pocketknife closing'. *Svenner* was the only major Allied warship lost on 6 June 1944. No German warships came anywhere near *Belfast*.

Above: 'We spread out, the three cruisers spread out along the beaches and it looked ever so peaceful after seeing all the fires and the bombing during the night,' – Denis Watkinson.
Watercolour by Stephen Bone, depicting soldiers on the deck of an LST.

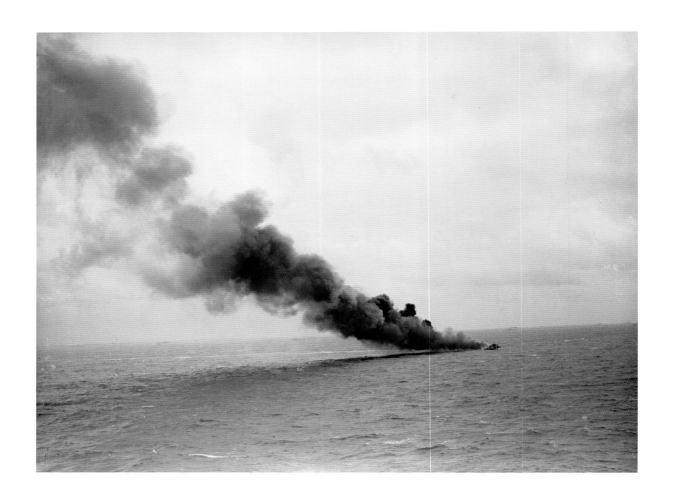

Above: 'You could see ... boats getting hit ... blowing up and flames in the water, things like that.'
— Denis Watkinson.
Photographed from the cruiser HMS *Frobisher*, a landing craft blows up and sinks after being hit by fire from a German shore battery.

Above: 'Warning E-boats NNE of Sword' — *Belfast*'s log, 8/9 June 1944.
A German *schnellboot* at speed at the end of the war. The British called them E-Boats, which stood for 'Enemy Boat'. German light coastal forces were the most serious naval threat faced by the Allied invasion armada. Boat-for-boat the German craft were superior to their Allied equivalents, although they were heavily outnumbered.

After nearly two hours of concentrated bombardment the first waves of assault troops went in at 07:25, after a last brief, devastating air raid. Tersely recorded as a log entry which read 'shore bombed' (Log 1), Charles Bunbury recorded the moment more dramatically in his journal:

At 07:10 waves of heavy bombers flew very high over the shore and plastered it with bombs, and during an air attack all the thousands of small craft made their way towards the shore. There were many LCRs, equipped with several hundred rockets, firing volleys of them on to the shore ... the first craft slid ashore at 07:30 ... There were machine gun nests returning fire and one or two large batteries still in action.

The rocket landing craft made an impression on nearly everyone who saw them. Larry Fursland watched them incinerate a wood, and the unfortunate German troops within it. 'Everything was going hammer and tongs', he remembered, 'They had a destroyer going along making black smoke, behind her was rocket ships, tank landing craft, flat bottomed ships with tubes that fire rockets. There couldn't have been a rat alive in that bloody woods.' Brian Butler was equally impressed: 'I've never seen anything like it. It just was motionless in the water [and] it began firing these rockets. It fired literally hundreds of them, the landing craft was just enveloped in a pall of smoke from end to end as these rockets were going off and they just set this wood afire from end to end.'

Butler's action station gave him a grandstand view. Like Gordon Painter, he was a sight-setter in one of the main 6-inch gun turrets, and although locked in for much of the time, he was still able to get the occasional glimpse of the outside world:

We went in right behind the minesweepers and took up our position there, and started to bombard the positions on shore. And this went on all day, we just bombarded and bombarded ... I was a local sight-setter in the turret just setting the range and the deflection and just doing my job ... The first day we were there for some hours and then we had a break and we were able

Above: Chalk drawing by war artist J C Heath, depicting a view from a landing craft approaching the shore. British soldiers are crouching in the boat which is surrounded by explosions and water plumes rising all around. Above the blazing shoreline, Allied aircraft are attacking targets near le Hamel.

to get out on the deck for a little while, get a bit of fresh air, get something to eat and I think we were allowed to pop down to the mess and go to the bathroom and that sort of thing, have a quick wash and then back up again.

This was Butler's day – relentless work from dawn until very late in the evening, broken only by these periodic 'comfort breaks', when he caught a glimpse, more of a snapshot, of what was going on outside:

We could see the landing craft going in and landing on the beaches and I remember one particular landing craft was hit by a shell and just disintegrated but ... the sea was still quite rough for people trying to get ashore ... there were thousands of small boats going hither and thither, and large ships ... further off the shore that they were coming from. They were just taking everything ashore and then the big tank landing craft came in as well and went in straight on to the beach.

For Charles Simpson and his men in *Belfast*'s engine room, deep inside the ship with no view of the outside world, it was hard to get a sense of what was going on. Ron Jesse was at his action station, manning the throttles in the forward engine room, when *Belfast* arrived. He found the whole experience distinctly underwhelming:

Left: 'Smoke. Smell of cordite which also smells rather like blood, and that smell wafted across the whole foreshore.' – Ron Jesse. The gloomy, smoke-shrouded shore of Juno Assault Area, near Bernières-sur-Mer, where much of the town had been set ablaze by the naval bombardment.

I had that morning watch and we were going ever so slowly on cruising engines, which is a cruising turbine clutched in front of the main turbines. [It] didn't use much fuel which is economical, but you normally would only use that for long distance. And we eventually arrived at our station and stopped and the first thing I thought was going to happen was that the chief engineer would instruct us to declutch the cruising engines. 'Oh no', he said, 'don't do that, stay where you are, we aren't going anywhere'. And I thought we were going to hare up and down at high speed blasting everything in sight, quite the opposite! We just stopped and then it started. Bang ... bang bang bang and then the announcement was made 'HMS *Belfast* fires the first shots in the relief of Europe' and it carried on for the next couple of hours pretty regular and determined and ... all we had to do was just keep manoeuvring to keep the ship faced at the correct angle to the shore ... and keep our position.

Even in the engine rooms, though, it was impossible to escape the relentless roar of the guns, although over time most men just got used to it, and then ignored it. Ron Jesse recalled 'a crash and a bang and a shudder, and a crash and a bang and a shudder, and a crash and a bang and a shudder ... you get used to until eventually if it goes on for a long time it fades into the background and you're just watching your duties and what you've got to do'. Fortunately, Ron Jesse worked for an empathetic, sensitive officer. Charles Simpson was well aware that the men under his command were making history, and yet almost entirely unable to get any sense of the scale of the operation they were contributing to. Intelligent enough to realise that *Belfast* was going to be almost stationary for a long time, he came up with a solution which allowed his men to get a sense of D-Day: 'I gave everybody in my engine room the opportunity … to go up for two minutes and have a look at what was going on.'

The necessarily brief opportunity seems to have focused the minds of Simpson's men, helping them take in as much as they could. For Ron Jesse, the first impression was smells, not sights: 'Smoke. Smell of cordite which also smells rather like blood and that smell wafted across the whole foreshore.' Looking more closely as the seconds ticked away, Jesse observed small buildings and a low foreshore, partly obscured by clouds of smoke and dust. Periodically, an enemy gun would flash on the skyline. Closer to hand, the landings were well underway: 'The landing craft were coming out of their parent landing ships … like ducklings from a nest and forming up and going ashore and the DUKWs, the ducks – the lorries which were waterproofed for sailing – they were going as well.' To his

Left: 'The DUKWs, the ducks – the lorries which were waterproofed for sailing – they were going as well.' – Ron Jesse. Loaded with ammunition, one of the famous DUKWs, or 'Ducks' leaves an LST and heads into the beaches. Although only intended as a temporary wartime expedient, DUKWs continued to be used after the war by the armies of several nations, and a few vintage 'Ducks' are still operating as tourist attractions.

horror, some of the DUKWS were swamped as he watched; although the gale had passed, the sea was still rough and choppy.

Once his men had had their two minutes, Charles Simpson himself went up on deck, as aware as everyone else that this was his one chance to watch history being made.

> I went last ... I can't describe the feeling. I saw a stretch of sandy beach, and a very rough sea. There were six, seven, eight foot waves rolling in towards the shore. On the shore was a row of houses and some trees ... and evidence of defence. There were millions of crossed bits of steel bars lying on the sand. In the sea there were innumerable infantry landing craft, some of which were so close to the *Belfast* that you could hear soldiers shouting a sort of cheer as they jumped into the waves. A great many of them vanished as they jumped. Then we could see a ... procession of soldiers carrying an immense amount of gear on their shoulders and on their back, slowly wending their way through the waves to the shoreline, where at the time we looked there were already a great number of soldiers. Some lying at the shoreline, some lying on the sand, a great many struggling on their knees up the sand. Some had just begun to reach the trees in front of the houses. But two minutes was two minutes so I came down.

Remarkably one young *Belfast* Able Seaman, Alan Jones, found time to scrawl a quick but nonetheless moving eyewitness letter to his family (now in IWM Department of Documents). As D-Day quite literally unfolded before his amazed eyes he wrote:

> As I am writing this, the sun is breaking dawn and it's a glorious day. As I look to my right I can see the green fields and small forests of Cherbourg [sic], which is just a mile away from the ship, and just over the hill you can see small bursts of smoke, where a kind of tank battle seems to be in progress ... we went in first with the invasion barges behind us, and then came the great moment when we opened fire. When we had finished shelling the beach, all the landing craft surged forward and landed on the beach and they seem to be making splendid progress ... If you were here right now you would be amazed at the number of ships there are here, and every now and again you can see streams of landing craft going ashore ... We shelled the German shore batteries and put nearly all of them out of action. We are just going to start another bombardment so I shall have to close now.

The staccato entries in Peter Brooke Smith's diary, compiled on the spot as he worked in the Director, provide one of the most dramatic accounts of the day: 'Very thrilling time now, engaging batteries. Shots from one falling between us and a destroyer, not more than three cables away, but always in the same hole. Then American mobile artillery in LCTs go in and give a splendid display while passing us.' However, Brooke Smith's diary is not a wholly exhaustive account. In a notebook maintained by Able Seaman Waterhouse in the Director Control Tower, between the relentless notes of 6-inch firings every minute or two, appears a brief scrawled line: 'cat had its breakfast 06:04 am!' The Director was sited high on *Belfast's* forward superstructure, on top of the former aircraft hangar. This could be uncomfortable, as Peter Brooke Smith noted: 'Interesting to watch progress. Destroyers now close inshore, belting away.

Above: Perhaps one of the most famous D-Day images, this still from the film *The True Glory* shows Canadian infantrymen of the North Shore (New Brunswick) Regiment disembarking from a Landing Craft Assault (LCA) onto Nan Red Beach, Juno Area, at la Rive, near St Aubin-sur-Mer, at about 08:05 hrs, while under fire from German troops in the houses facing them.

We fire in spasms. Occasionally necessary to train our director round to get out of blast from our own guns – fortunately headphones protect my ears … Our day most unsatisfactory as couldn't get in touch with our FOB.'

The FOB (Forward Observation Bombardment), was *Belfast's* observer ashore. Once the first, preregistered targets – like La Marefontaine battery – had been neutralised, *Belfast* and other bombarding ships essentially became floating artillery, at the disposal of the troops ashore. But in the confusion of battle, with friendly and enemy forces locked in combat, perhaps only a few metres from each other, the ship needed more precise information than could be obtained from Peter Brooke Smith's rangefinders, which were designed to fight a battle against enemy ships –

Above: 'We shelled the German shore batteries and put nearly all of them out of action. We are just going to start another bombardment so I shall have to close now.' – Alan Jones. In a still taken from the Hollywood director George Stevens' remarkable colour film, HMS *Belfast's* 6-inch guns blast the Normandy coast in the grey early morning light of 6 June 1944.

essentially isolated targets set in miles and miles of empty ocean, with very little risk of what is today euphemistically dubbed 'friendly fire'. *Belfast* had therefore been assigned a Royal Artillery Bombardment Liaison Officer. The BLO was in constant radio contact with the FOB ashore, who had the dangerous task of spotting for the guns and transmitting back targeting information.

The FOB had a small team of Royal Navy and army personnel, and their work was extremely dangerous. Some, like Telegraphist Wilf Fortune, were dropped into action with the paratroops and their experiences were essentially those of front line infantry:

> I crossed the bridge just as the seaborne troops crossed, and the Paras pointed them out in a wood across this cornfield, but they warned me about snipers. I zig-zagged across expecting a sniper's bullet at any time, but I made it and found Vere [Captain Vere Hodge, Royal Artillery] and Alex [Leading Telegraphist Alex Boomer]. Alex was signalling to the ships by Morse Code to send the shells over. We had our position and the position of the enemy, and we telegraphed that to the ship by Morse. Then the officer would give his 'Fall of Shot'. This was a reference to the target which is at the centre of the clock face, the FOB is at six o'clock. Then 'Direction of Fall of Shot Landing', A equals 100 yards, B equals 200 yards, etc ... the ship had an artillery officer on board, but the ship also had to get itself in position for the shot so it might be ten minutes before anything happened. Then there would be the call from the ship, 'Fire for Effect', and the ranging shells would come over.

Belfast's FOB disappeared for quite some time, which given the hazards of his work was hardly surprising, but as the 'buzz' spread around the lower deck, many aboard were convinced he had been killed. Larry Fursland even recalled his name: 'We had a liaison officer ashore called Bobby, I could hear the ship saying "come in Bobby, come in Bobby"... no answer. So Bobby might have got killed or injured so somebody had to take over.' Ordinary Seaman Bert Brown was a 20-year-old Canadian, part of a group seconded to *Belfast* to gain experience of

Below: 'Our day most unsatisfactory as couldn't get in touch with our FOB.' – Peter Brooke Smith. A spotting team from an FOB unit at work in one of the forward observation posts in the Sword Area. Over a hundred FOB officers were deployed on D-Day, each with his own team of seven communications ratings. Initially they landed with a crude portable wireless on a cart, replacing this with progressively more sophisticated equipment and better transport once the beaches were secure.

service in bigger ships – not a pleasant experience according to Brown, like his comrades more used to the informality of the Royal Canadian Navy's corvettes and other small escort ships. He, too, recalled 'Bobby':

Robert Brown

> We sent a signalman ashore and he met up with a soldier and a jeep and they went in as forward observers and signalled back to the ship ... They would call the fall of shot and report when they asked for broadside and find out where they'd hit and report the number of tanks that we'd hit or the number of trucks that we'd hit. They had a scoreboard that they kept on the ship so we knew that we were doing some good.

It was not just the men in the turrets who were slaves to the voracious appetites of the guns, as *Belfast* relentlessly pounded the smoke-shrouded shore. Five decks down from Brian Butler and Gordon Painter, 20-year-old Bernard Thomson was sweltering in the cruiser's shell room, mechanically feeding ammunition into the hoists which took the shells and cordite charges up to the turrets. Less than a year earlier, he had been working in the Ford factory in Dagenham – now he was playing a small part in the liberation of occupied Europe. Thomson's 'day job' on board could not have been more different – he was an Officers' Cook – but now he was handling lethal explosives. When *Belfast* went to action stations on the morning of 6 June, he followed his mess mates down the steep steel ladders to the shell rooms, deep down in the ship, below the waterline and behind the armoured belt, with no natural light and precious little ventilation. There he stayed, for the next three days:

Bernard Thomson

> When we got to Normandy we certainly knew the guns were firing that day. There were broadsides going off ... and shells were going from the magazine and everything, and very little time for rest ... we had to just lay down on the steel floor in the magazine. I would take the shells out of special racks ... and place them on to a ... revolving wheel which used to go round in a big circle, it would be about seven feet wide. There would be another rating in the centre of that circle, he would push them up into a pipe ... with a little door on and that had like a lift and that used to take them up to the gun ... Sometimes you used to write little messages on the shells 'there's one for you' or some rude words.

After 24 hours, broken only by a few fitful naps on the hard steel deck, Thomson was ordered to descend one deck further, into the ship's

Above: 'We sent a signalman ashore and he met up with a soldier and a jeep and they went in as forward observers and signalled back to the ship' — Robert Brown.
Royal Navy telegraphists man a wireless set at a Forward Observation Bombardment unit headquarters, possibly located in an abandoned German bunker in the Sword Area. From here, spotting teams were sent forward, messages passed back to ships, and 'shoots' co-ordinated.

magazine, where the cordite propellant charges were stored. *Belfast*'s 6-inch guns did not use 'cased' ammunition, with the propellant (which sent the shell flying towards its destination) and the explosive charge (which caused the damage at the other end) in a single sealed unit. Instead, every time the gun was fired, the shell and the cordite charge had to be inserted separately. Cordite was extremely volatile, and every precaution had to be taken to minimise the risk of an accident which could destroy the ship and kill everyone aboard:

> I was told to take my jacket off and my shoes, I didn't know what was going on and all I had on was me socks and me underpants and me vest. He opened this big hatch door and he said 'go in there and put that cordite into the chute ... when that cordite moves up, you take another one out of that big case over there ... and place it in there and pull that little lever and wait until that goes and then you put another one and he locked me in with a key.

Thomson was alone, buried deep inside the ship, surrounded by lethal cordite charges. Years later, he freely admitted that he had been 'terrified':

Left: 'An asbestos cloth hood which covered most of your face except eyes, mouth and nose, and gloves which covered up to above your elbows, also of asbestos material, and it was solely that if there was an explosion in the vicinity the flash could do you more harm than the actual physical force of the explosion.' – Ron Jesse.
Another George Stevens still. Shrouded in anti-flash gear, *Belfast*'s crew clear away cordite cases on the morning of 6 June.

I knew that if anything had happened to him he had the key and I couldn't get out. As a matter of fact, to get out of the magazine was a hard job in any case because you was three or four decks down below and you had to go through two main hatches to get up anyway. I was down there for two or three days and the food was coming down ... iron rations and sandwiches and mugs of tea and mugs of coffee and sometimes cocoa at night times.

Up on the bridge, Wireless Operator Len Beardsley was continuing resolutely with his job in the face of considerable distractions. It is, perhaps, the true secret behind the success of D-Day – the largest, most complex, military operation in modern history was made up of hundreds of thousands of individuals, each carrying out his or her own small, often monotonous or mundane task to the best of their ability, never questioning its importance or its relevance to the ultimate goal. It was a generation raised on the concept of 'duty', which sometimes might involve sitting in a noisy, stifling and dark little room with headphones on, rather than storming the beaches or shooting down Messerschmitts:

Above: 'All I saw was just landing craft and soldiers going backwards and forwards in up the beach with supplies and tanks rolling up the beach and reinforcements and suchlike.' – Len Beardsley. Sherman tanks of 'A' Squadron, Nottinghamshire Yeomanry (Sherwood Rangers), 8th Armoured Brigade, come ashore from a landing craft, LCT 1076, on Jig Beach, Gold Area, 6 June 1944. On the right a bulldozer is clearing a path off the beach.

The ship used to shudder as soon as the guns started, everything shuddered and then crash, boom-boom ... it was quite horrendous really but you just on with it ... I was hoping my radio wouldn't pack up with all the shaking ... as long as I could hear that signal, and that was my job: to read that Admiralty signal coming through and [to write] down the messages and pass them on. That was my job, as long as I did my job that was it, and they were doing their job the gunnery people ... making a dreadful noise.

Although Beardsley was high up in the forward bridge superstructure, he 'couldn't see a thing', partly because of the need to concentrate on the task in hand, but partly because the view was becoming increasingly obscured by smoke from gunfire and the many fires which the ship's log records having started ashore (Log 1). 'It was only afterwards', he remembered years later, '[once] the landing was a success and so on, that we could get out on the upper deck and view the situation, view all the French coastline. Even then you couldn't see anything, all I saw was just landing craft and soldiers going backwards and forwards in up the beach with supplies and tanks rolling up the beach and reinforcements and suchlike'.

As the soldiers waded ashore, Captain Parham left the bridge for the first time in hours, albeit only to go one deck down into the chart house to check on progress and plan his next targets. In the chart house, a loudspeaker was broadcasting (what else) the BBC, providing Parham with a wonderful moment of typically British whimsy:

> As I came down into the chart house at about ten minutes past seven on the morning of what I suppose was really one of the greatest, most important days in the whole history of the Empire, a voice from the loudspeaker said 'Now then girls are we all ready? Let's stretch the arms, let's stretch the legs'. It was May Brown doing the morning exercises. Really, honestly, what a country!

Belfast's log records constant 6-inch firing throughout the morning, broken up by the occasional piece of news from shore, including the capture of the strategically vital Mont Fleury Battery, another of *Belfast*'s targets, at 09:30 (Log 1). Mont Fleury, another unfinished installation begun after Rommel's inspection like la Marefontaine, was famously captured almost single-handedly by Company Sergeant-Major Stan Hollis of D Company, 6th Battalion, The Green Howards, who for this and other heroic actions was awarded the only Victoria Cross of D-Day. The log also records the occasional air raid warning; like the Kriegsmarine, the once-mighty Luftwaffe was a shadow of its former self, but it is nevertheless a common misapprehension that it had virtually ceased to exist by 1944. Air attacks, usually directed against the fleet, were a constant, wearying threat and, although hindsight tells us reassuringly that they were not of a scale capable of posing any kind of serious threat to the invasion, this was small comfort to the individual sailors on the receiving end, including the *Belfast* men, who were treated to a stick of bombs off the starboard beam at 10:00.

As the morning wore on, the Corncob blockships began to edge their way painstakingly towards the shore, where they were scuttled in a long, irregular line to form the protective breakwater which constituted the first phase of the Mulberry harbour. Second Officer Lester Everett was the Navigating and Gunnery Officer aboard one of them, the SS *Empire Moorhen*, an American-built cargo ship of First World War vintage.

Above: Gun crews try to keep their feet on the rolling, slippery decks of an LCF (Landing Craft Flak) off Courseulles-sur-Mer, in Juno Area, 6 June 1944. LCFs were converted LCTs, with the ramp welded shut and a deck built on top of the tank decks, on which were mounted light anti-aircraft guns, typically eight 20mm Oerlikon and four 2-pounder (40mm) 'pom-poms'.

Left: Vertical aerial reconnaissance photograph of the landings on Mike Beach, Juno Area, at Courseulles-sur-Mer, 6 June 1944. Landing ships can be seen pulled up on the beach to the right, and the scene is dominated by the meandering path of the River Seulles, becoming more regular in form as it morphs into the town's quayside and wharves. HMS *Belfast* was operating off this area.

Above: A striking aerial view of the outer Gooseberry line of blockships, now reinforced by Phoenix breakwaters. The importance of the Mulberry harbour is clearly illustrated by the state of the water — still and calm inside the breakwater where the ships and smaller craft are safely anchored, it is much rougher outside.

Before sailing, the ship had been stripped of all extraneous fixtures and fittings, and explosive charges had been laid in each of her five holds, connected to a firing point on the bridge. Arriving off Arromanches, Everett ordered the anchor dropped and the *Empire Moorhen* ended her final journey, at the end of a long line of similarly superannuated freighters. Responsibility for the next phase passed to a sinister-sounding character known as the 'wrecking officer': 'After a short while we were boarded by the "wrecking officer" and his party, and without further ado the aforementioned cables running to the bridge were connected to a plunger, the trigger was pressed and Number 307 [*Empire Moorhen's* blockship designation] sank gently on to the bed of the English Channel in about 2½ fathoms of water, close inshore at Arromanches'.

Unknowingly, Brian Butler was experiencing the kind of coincidence which only happens in wartime or Hollywood:

> My brother ... he was a DEMS [Defensively Equipped Merchant Ships] gunner and he was on ... a very old merchant ship ... His was one of the ships they ran in on to the beach to form a temporary harbour to unload things off, until they got the Mulberry harbours built and he was ashore there and he knew I was out there on the *Belfast* because he recognised the *Belfast*. I had no idea that he was there and our guns were firing straight over the top of his ship and he said they were like express trains going by ... we never met until after the war.

Left: 'My brother ... his was one of the ships they ran in on to the beach to form a temporary harbour ... he knew I was out there on the *Belfast* because he recognised the *Belfast* ... he said they were like express trains going by' – Brian Butler. Chalk drawing by war artist Stephen Bone, showing the Corncob blockships at high water, with only their masts and upperworks visible.

Top left: 'How they built the Mulberry harbour ... it was really brilliant the way they did that.' — Bob Shrimpton.
A row of Beetle pontoons and Whale floating roadways being towed across a choppy English Channel to form part of the Mulberry harbour at Arromanches. The roadway units were towed in standard groups of five. They were not easy to tow, especially in rough weather, and several sank on the way across.

Bottom left: A 7,000 ton concrete Phoenix caisson being manoeuvred into position in the main breakwater off the coast at Arromanches. The men on top give an indication of the enormous size of these units, whilst the presence of at least three tugs gives some idea of the complexity of the operations involved every time one had to be placed.

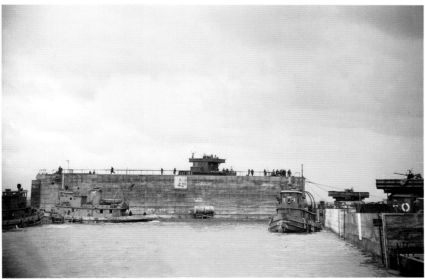

Belfast was one of the larger warships with a fully equipped sick bay, plus a qualified surgeon, Surgeon-Commander J H Nicholson, supported by two Surgeon Lieutenants, Horne and Watson (both pre-war professionals serving 'for the duration' in the Royal Naval Volunteer Reserve). As the day wore on a trickle of casualties began to arrive on board, the first at 13:00, as *Belfast* manoeuvred closer to the shore to try and re-establish contact with her FOB. Charles Bunbury recorded the moment in his journal: 'Their LCT had struck a mine and these men were rather badly wounded. Two of them died that night.' For many *Belfast* men, this was their first shocking, direct exposure to the brutal reality of modern warfare. Peter Brooke Smith described 'the calmness of [a] stretcher case lighting cigarette, [with the] look in his face of one who had known what he was going to be up against'.

War Correspondent Rex North apparently remembered the same man as he prepared his piece for the *Sunday Pictorial* (Peter Brooke Smith

Above: Mulberry B at Arromanches in its full, extraordinary glory. In the background are the sunken Gooseberry blockships and a line of Phoenix breakwaters. Closer to shore, Spud pierheads with their distinctive adjustable legs are already in position, and a long Whale roadway stretches back to the shore, supported by Beetle pontoons. Landing craft and other small vessels are sheltering inside, and larger ships are discharging cargo at the pierheads.

reproduced North's article in full – according to his transcript, it was dated 11 June 1944 and bylined 'On Board HMS *Belfast*'.) North recalled the circumstances in some detail. 'There is one face I shall never forget', he wrote, apparently genuinely moved, 'we had slunk through the waters of the channel. We had fired the first shot of the invasion bombardment, but still it is the face of one man that I think about'. North painted a vivid picture of the dramatic moment when the Fairmile motor launch *ML 297* drew alongside:

'Will you take an injured man on board?' we were asked. We lowered a drawer, from a large cupboard, on the end of a crane. I know it sounds very simple. But just try to picture it with me now. The sea was white-lipped, angry and rough. The small craft was being heaved nose first into the air as methodically as if somewhere down there at the bottom of the sea a piston was beating to time. Every time they reached for the makeshift stretcher,

Above: 'He said that for three years he had been in the army ... training, training and then training some more for D-Day, and now this had happened.' – Rex North, *Sunday Pictorial.*
A shaken, wounded soldier is helped aboard the cruiser HMS *Frobisher*, watched by members of the ship's company. Such sobering scenes were repeated all around the fleet on 6 June 1944, including aboard HMS *Belfast*.

the boat sank in the pit between the waves, and all the while a man was bleeding profusely because part of his leg was blown away when his landing craft struck a mine. He lay on that deck, a cigarette stuck between his lips, his eyes wide open, watching and wondering whether the stretcher would dash him in the face, but still trying to smile.

As the grievously wounded soldier was slowly swung inboard, North greeted him, inadequately but understandably, with a murmured 'bad luck old man.' The soldier smiled but could not speak. 'Later, just before his legs were amputated, he said that for three years he had been in the army … training, training and then training some more for D-Day, and now this had happened.'

Signaller Lance Tyler recalled Captain Parham's extraordinary compassion. Even at the height of the battle, probably one of the busiest and most stressful times of his professional life, he still found time to check on the terribly young, wounded soldiers who were suddenly in his care:

> I think at this stage he was only about 40 or 42 [and] he was in charge of HMS *Belfast* which was quite a responsibility, but while we were over France I had a great deal of time for him. He sent me down to the sick bay on D-Day itself because he knew that an army corporal had been badly blown up and they were trying to save this man's life, and the fact that he had enough time to spare to think about other people, I reckon that's one of the ways in which he eventually became a full admiral.

Sadly, compassion alone was not enough to save the lives of men whose bodies had sometimes been so dreadfully mangled. A grim note in the ship's log records: '22:15 Gunner Mayo died on board' (Log 1). This was almost certainly Rifleman Cyril Mayo of the Royal Winnipeg Rifles, a Canadian soldier from Selkirk, Manitoba. *Belfast* was operating along the divide between Gold beach and the Canadian beach, Juno, providing fire support to both forces. Two hours later, just after midnight, another seriously wounded soldier died on board, Private Kenneth Young of The Hampshire Regiment – recorded by the Commonwealth War Graves Commission as the 20-year-old son of Victor and Marjorie Young of Gosport, Hampshire. For the *Belfast* men, death in action was no longer an abstract concept. The Canadian seaman Bert Brown witnessed the melancholy end of the story: 'I remember seeing a Bosun stitching a body up in canvas.'

Larry Fursland witnessed another critically wounded casualty, an unidentified soldier from the Royal Artillery who also apparently later died: 'I remember one ... I was going on watch and he had Royal Artillery on him. He made the V-sign. They took his legs away ... and the Master-at-Arms ditched them over the side in canvas ... He was covered in blood [and] I know they put him over the side.' But for Fursland, it was the sight of dead bodies in the water which he found most distressing, particularly as no-one appeared to be making any attempt to recover them. Eventually, after hours of watching naval picket boats bump gently up to body after body, and the men aboard lean over to remove identity discs but then leaving the dead to bob miserably in the water, he was unable to restrain himself any longer, and protested to one of his officers that it was 'bloody disgusting'. The officer's response was chilling:

'Don't you realise Fursland', he said. I said, 'No, tell me'. He said 'if a body gets washed up on the shore they get a burial, but you get a flood tide of six hours and an ebb tide of six hours. If you don't finish [recovering identity discs] that flood tide the further and further they go out on the ebb tides [and] the body dismembers'.

The young Coppersmith, Ron Jesse, suddenly became involved in an intensely personal way in the treatment of another badly wounded Canadian:

Below: 'They took his legs away ... He was covered in blood.' — Larry Fursland. Chalk drawing by war artist J C Heath, depicting a beach dressing station with two rows of injured British soldiers, one being given a drip by medical personnel. Medical facilities on the beach on 6 June were basic, and doctors aimed to patch up casualties as quickly as possible, then move them out to the waiting ships and back to the UK.

There was a chap brought off, a Canadian who'd been two years training in Canada for this day, and he'd come across and waited his time and gone across on the first wave of landing craft, stepped on a mine and had to be brought straight off. He came back to the *Belfast* where he had severe damage to his foot and I was asked to make a device which would put a wire through his heel bone for pulling him out straight again by screwing this mechanism ... I worked like frenzy at this to get it done in time for the surgeon to pull his leg out and hold it out while he screwed and splinted it. That was my only experience of death and casualties.

Rex North was not the only guest aboard *Belfast*; the cruiser was also hosting the US film director George Stevens, officially present to record the D-Day landings for the US Army Signals Corps. In addition to filming the Normandy landings, his unit went on to shoot the liberation of Paris and of Dachau; the footage was used as evidence in the Nuremberg trials. After the war he was responsible for productions such as *Shane*, *The Diary of Ann Frank* and *Giant*. On *Belfast*, Stevens had also brought along a 16mm hand-held camera for his own use. The resulting footage is the only known colour film of *Belfast* taken during the Second World War.

As the casualties came aboard, gradually the battle ashore started to turn in the Allies' favour. At 13:26, a note in the log records that four coastal towns, including Ver-sur-Mer, were now in Allied hands (Log 1). Gradually, those men who were able to see what was going on started

Above: 'I went up on the upper deck on one occasion, we were receiving the wounded soldiers coming back from the beach ... all I saw was the bloodstained bandages and them lying on stretchers.' – Len Beardsley. Weary Commandos of 4 Commando, 1st Special Service Brigade, use an improvised stretcher to bring one of their casualties back as they advance into Ouistreham, Sword Area, 6 June 1944.

Above: 'We were actually anchored off the coast of Normandy, I suppose about 5 miles out
or something like that, this coast which had been denied to us for over 5 years.' – Captain
Frederick Parham.
Belfast's bridge team, with one of George Stevens' camera crew in the background, 6 June 1944.

to get a sense that the battle might just be going well. Bob Shrimpton, still ensconced as a lookout high up on the bridge, was one of them:

> You couldn't see any movement on beaches, you saw ... supply lorries and tanks going ashore and they'd just disappear off. And there was not the volume of gunfire and the rattle of small arms, that was way in the distance, so you realised that they'd gone farther inland. And then of course you'd get the reports coming over the radio from the Home Service ... and they were keeping you up to date because they knew more about it than we did from their forward position. So that was how it gradually disappeared ... it was a strange sort of feeling. Because you'd been so highly tensed up, coming up to before the landing and then the actual landing and now it's like ... a deflated balloon. You thought what else is there for us to do now?

There was, of course, still plenty to do, and night brought little respite. The relentless bombardment continued, and the onset of darkness increased the fear of air attack. The fleet's gunners were jumpy, and *Belfast*'s log records eight air-raid warnings between 17:55 and the end

Above: 'I'm very proud to have been part of it. Very proud indeed.' – Bob Shrimpton.
HMS *Belfast* in action off the beaches of Normandy, seen from the upper deck of another ship in this oil painting by Frank Russell Flint. The cruiser is firing her forward guns at the smoke-shrouded French coast in choppy seas, surrounded by landing craft and other small craft.

of 6 June. Several turned out to be actual raids, including a major attack at 18:56 which started a large fire and huge clouds of smoke on the beach, and 'a tip and run' raid at 23:35, the last of D-Day, in the course of which HMS *Emerald* was damaged by splinters from a shell which exploded nearby and a stick of bombs fell close alongside *Belfast*'s port side (Log 1). Peter Brooke Smith recorded that 'Everything in the anchorage panicked and opened fire, wonderful tracer display. Some bombs dropped. Spent night at second degree of AA readiness'. For Brooke Smith, this meant a snatched three hours of sleep inside his Director, where he was also able to listen to King George VI's 'impressive' speech.

Food meant 'action messing', a hastily served snack delivered to the men at their action stations. Denis Watkinson ate beside his 4-inch gun: 'They used to make kai which is cocoa, they used to make a bath full and you used to take the fanny down ... to the galley, fill it full of cocoa and bring it on the gun. That's all you had. And they had hardtack ... I'm sure they were dog biscuits! We had a couple of them, but we had to wait.' Later the NAAFI canteen was opened for men to run down and grab extra rations. Chocolate was particularly popular, as in normal circumstances this treat would have to be paid for! Watkinson managed to acquire so much that 'when I went home afterward I had a little case ... and it was full of... Frys chocolate bars ... I took a lot home for my mother!'

For Captain Parham, the evening provided an opportunity for reflection: 'I shall never ever forget', he said many years later, 'it was about five or six o'clock that evening. We were actually anchored off the coast of Normandy, I suppose about five miles out or something like that, this coast which had been denied to us for over five years.'

The liberation of Occupied north-west Europe had begun, and HMS *Belfast* had survived her 'longest day'.

Above: 'I do remember seeing the old Dakotas flying over, towing the Horsa gliders; that was quite a sight to see.' – Bob Shrimpton. Officers and men on the bridge of the frigate HMS *Holmes* watch gliders passing overhead, carrying reinforcements for the 6th Airborne Division to defend the eastern flank of the invasion area along the Caen Canal and the Orne River, on the evening of 6 June 1944.

CHAPTER FIVE
LIFE ON THE GUNLINE
'8 June 13:45 *Belfast* ordered to destroy a town' – Log 1

After the excitement of 6 June, Operation 'Neptune' settled into a relentless pattern of bombardment duties during the day, and 'alarms and excursions' during the night for the *Belfast* men, with little to distinguish one day from another. The ship's log helps thread together what tend to be quite disjointed memories into a consistent narrative.

The command challenge for Parham was an unusual one. D-Day was not a naval action like the Battle of North Cape, with a clear beginning and end. Although the threat levels gradually diminished, there was no point at which he could state with certainty that it was 'over'. However, keeping the entire ship's company at action stations for weeks at a time was clearly impractical, not just because the men would soon become totally exhausted and demoralised, but also because it was essential to release them to carry out the routine maintenance and domestic tasks on which the ship depended. Consequently, from 7 June Parham divided the ship's company in half into two large watches, Red Watch and Blue Watch, which would alternately remain at action stations and return to normal duties, or 'cruising stations'. For Bernard Thomson, it was finally time to leave his action station in the magazine. It is only too easy to imagine him emerging, blinking, on to the upper deck, and peering through the drizzle and low cloud to watch, probably with amazement, Operation 'Overlord' unfolding around him:

> We went back to normal duties and half the ship would stay at action stations and the other half would carry on with jobs on the ship which had to be maintained ... and I was amazed at all the ships that were around in the distance and all that, and the firing. They were firing while I was working and I saw the soldiers on the beaches and ... there was these big pontoons full of soldiers sitting on them, at least two to three hundred of them being pulled ashore by ... a small craft. There was one or two of them and they were going into shore and the poor soldiers they looked terrified. I waved to them but they didn't wave back. I was up on deck at that time, I wanted to shout but I didn't know what to do.

Given the circumstances, the resumption of ordinary shipboard life seems almost incongruous. For Thomson, it meant returning to his duties as an Officers' Cook:

> The likes of me and the stewards had to cook for the officers ... As an officers' cook we had a separate galley, I used to be in the galley for the

Left: In another famous D-Day photograph, an infantry-laden Cromwell Mk IV tank of 4th County of London Yeomanry, 22nd Armoured Brigade, 7th Armoured Division, comes ashore from the Royal Navy tank landing ship LST 406, Gold Area, June 1944. 406's story was fairly typical – built in Baltimore, Maryland, she never saw service with the US Navy but was transferred to the UK under lend-lease. At the end of the war she was returned to the USA.

main officers. There used to be the Chief Chef, a Petty Officer, a killick [Leading Seaman], and two ordinary cooks. Now next door, there were three little galleys together, only mesh separated them. Next door was what they called the Captain's Galley. There was a Petty Officer Cook in there only, used to cook for the Captain and his guest. Now and again I used to help out in there ... there was another little galley to the offside of us and that used to look after 20 midshipmen ... My galley was at the after end near X Turret and Y Turret, near the torpedo tubes. You walked into a teeny little passageway and it's like a room there's a bulkhead on the offside with portholes in and the rest is wire mesh for ventilation.

Thomson's experience perfectly illustrates the paradox of naval life. Unlike soldiers, sailors took their homes with them to war, and never had to entirely forsake domestic comfort for the rigours of a front-line existence. Perhaps this explains why despite the risks of a cold lonely death at sea, or sudden immolation in a catastrophic explosion, most sailors would not have exchanged their experience for that of a soldier, living in a hole in the ground on cold bully beef. The contrast provided some amusement – overnight, Thomson had exchanged high explosives for the considerably less risky threat posed by a temperamental oil-fired range:

It used to be a terrible job to start in the morning. You used to have to turn two taps, the air jet and the fuel jet, and you used to get a little bit of ... wire wool and you used to light it, adjust it and thrown it in and hope for the best ... sometimes it go off like a big firework and blow back on you!'

Whilst undoubtedly easier than two days in the shell rooms, being a cook was still hard work. If he was on the breakfast shift, Thomson's routine began at 05:00, when the duty Royal Marine would come into the mess deck to call the duty cooks, identifying them easily enough because 'you used to hang something off your hammock to let them know you were the one they wanted'. Some of the Marines were less than sympathetic: 'They used to have the army stick, some of these Marines, and they used to come up and give you a little twist on the hammock and nearly tip you out, or they used to give you a dig up the backside.' Instead of handling volatile cordite charges, Thomson was back to manipulating rather less threatening but no less vital substances – fried bread pyramids or the officers' favourite, liver croutons:

A typical breakfast for the officers was usually bacon, egg and beans or something like that, or sometimes you make liver croutons ... it was liver, mixed up, cooked and [we] added a little bit of ingredients and pepper and salt, made like mincemeat only 'pastified' and we used to fry bread in nice little shapes and we used to put it on like a pyramid and shove them in the oven for a couple of minutes ... They used to love that for their breakfast ... Then you prepared a lunch ... and they would have soup, vegetables and meat ... After lunch you'd start preparing for the evening dinner.

But although for a while the greatest threat Thomson faced on a daily basis was the fearsome Chief Cook ('he used to walk round like a peacock in his lovely white uniform, he didn't get his hands dirty, he just used to give orders'), for *Belfast*, the shooting war still continued. 7 June began, like so many days, with dawn air-raid alerts at 04:15, followed, at 06:15, by an actual attack when a pair of Focke-Wulf 190 fighter bombers swooped to make a long, diving run across the anchorage. One dropped a bomb on the headquarters ship HMS *Bulolo*, which was anchored nearby, causing several casualties and starting a fire. Andy Palmer was now working as Air Defence Controller, trying to bring some order and discipline to the fleet's anti-aircraft gunnery. This was not an easy task. Most airmen remember sailors with some venom as trigger-happy bandits, although in their defence, many sailors had spent years in the cross hairs of Luftwaffe bomb sights and had long ago learned that where unidentified aircraft were concerned it was safer to shoot first and ask questions later. The 7 June attack was fairly typical, as Palmer recalled with some frustration: 'Not a ship in the anchorage, not a ship, opened fire on those two damned aircraft. About half a mile astern of them they were being chased by two Spitfires and I think every ship opened fire on them in spite of my appealing on the radio.' So much for the famous 'D-Day stripes' that Mountifield had explained in the lecture attended by Charles Bunbury just a few days earlier.

Belfast opened fire with her 6-inch guns at 09:40 on 7 June and remained in action for the rest of the day, on and off. Her log records constant firing until 13:50, broken up by situation reports from ashore, including the welcome news at 12:30 that the Americans were entering the key town of Bayeux and 47 Commando, Royal Marines, were close to seizing the coastal town of Port-en-Bessin. The ship then ceased fire to shift position, before opening fire again from 14:20 until 15:15, and then again until well into the night; the last recorded 'shoot' on 7 June finished at 22:35. It was hard for the *Belfast* men, even Parham, to really know what exactly they were shooting at, although a brief note in the log at 21:35 confirms 'German infantry dispersed' (Log 1). Soon afterwards, *Belfast*'s over-enthusiastic gunners inflicted one of the ship's few D-Day wounds, when blast from her own guns damaged the bridge, just above the little compartment where Len Beardsley was sitting, still steadfastly noting down his admiralty signals:

> I recollect ... there being a loud clattering from up above on the upper deck and I thought 'what the hell can that be?' Some of the guys said it sounds like machine gun bullets, somebody's attacking us ... or it could have been a shell with shrapnel hitting us or something of that sort ... I never did discover what the dreadful noise was, so once again I put my earphones back on and got on with my job.

Boy Seaman David Jones was on deck at the time and saw the incident:

> Above the twin 4-inch guns where we were there was an eight barrelled pom-pom. It had an inverted funnel put on the end of the barrel, called a flash eliminator. One of these came off, while they were blazing away ... and a shell from one of other guns hit it and exploded and wounded a bloke who was on the upper deck nearby. His name was Steel, I remember him.

Occasional self-inflicted wounds aside, the ship's deadly work, so thrilling on 6 June, soon became routine, almost dull according to George Burridge: 'Quite close to [routine] because we weren't involved in any opposition so we were simply standing off the Caen area and the 6-inch guns were continuously firing ... on a controlled basis depending on what the army wanted. But ... it got quite close to being routine.' Apparently it even became possible to accept the relentless booming of the guns, Burridge recalling matter of factly that 'you got used to [the noise]'... it was very very noisy certainly'. Although the usual routine was to fire one or two turrets together, at times on 7 June *Belfast* fired full broadsides of all twelve 6-inch guns simultaneously, when according to Bernard Thomson the ship tilted, and there was 'a little rock afterwards'. The Canadian, Bert Brown, also remembered that broadsides 'would actually move the ship sideways in the water'. Brown was another man who got used to the noise, although the long-term damage to his hearing was so

severe that years later the Canadian Department for Veterans' Affairs awarded him a pension as compensation.

At 18:30, the log records a sad little ritual, when a boat from the cruiser HMS *Orion* arrived alongside and *Belfast*'s pitiful cargo of wounded soldiers were gently transferred, along with the bodies of Privates Mayo and Young, doubtless for transfer back to the UK or to a proper hospital ship (Log 1). Peter Brooke Smith cryptically noted in his diary that amongst the wounded soldiers was 'the imperturbable one', presumably the stretcher case he had observed earlier.

7 June ended like D-Day itself, with an air-raid alert, fires on land and the anchorage vividly illuminated by tracer fire from anti-aircraft guns ashore and on the warships. According to Brooke Smith it was 'a great show ... but ships less indiscriminate than last night'. Parham took his ship to seaward for the night, and ordered a smokescreen to be laid, a sensible precaution given the continued threat from German aircraft

Above: 'It was a bit wearing you know, shells exploding here and there.' – David Jones.
This oil painting by Stephen Bone shows the busy, crowded Normandy shore, as seen from high up on a ship. On the right a laden LST is making its way slowly across the anchorage. Behind, a German shell has narrowly missed one of dozens of anchored freighters.

and E-Boats. The ship's log records a busy night, with an E-boat alert at 02:44, a warning of enemy destroyers within 15 miles at 03:20, and an air raid ashore at 03:40 (Log 1). Nevertheless, the smoke did little to improve conditions for his men. According to Denis Watkinson 'it was terrible cos it was all getting inside the ship ... it does make you cough and that ... if you get in an enclosed space. It's not so bad if it's spread around but anyway we survived'. Doubtless the piping of 'up spirits' (an issue of rum) did much to alleviate the discomfort.

Belfast came back inshore on the morning of 8 June and anchored off Juno, beginning another day's ritual of bombarding and shifting berth, bombarding and shifting berth. The cold logic of the log entries at times has a chilling quality, as in: '8 June 13:45 *Belfast* ordered to destroy a town' (Log 1). Twenty minutes later more casualties came aboard, victims of an accident witnessed by Peter Brooke Smith, who had left his Director and was spending his free time on the after control deck, learning how to fire a 20mm Oerlikon anti-aircraft gun. Ashore, he could see sappers from the Royal Engineers methodically clearing the hundreds of mines and other explosive devices which the Germans had left attached to beach obstacles. As he watched, there was a huge explosion in the direction of Ouistreham, 'as if an oil tank had gone up', and almost immediately a disaster much closer to home when a 'Landing craft blows up and disintegrates 200 yards away'. Brooke Smith watched aghast as a hopelessly fumbled rescue ensued: 'Poor rescue work by a motor boat, while a soldier in a Duck motored up to the scene, ignored survivors and salvaged a box instead!' *Belfast* tried to help but the ship's performance was no better, according to Brooke Smith, who wrote that 'of course, our cutter was lowered into the water only when everything was over. The turning out and lowering gear is hopelessly inefficient'.

Three Royal Marines were killed in the incident, and another three badly wounded survivors were eventually brought aboard *Belfast*. As it turned out, the entire dreadful accident was an avoidable consequence of poor safety precautions by a group of overworked men, exhausted after two days spent dismantling lethal explosive devices, as the log explains: 'Evidently sappers ashore had given the Royal Marines some German land mines to ditch and they had exploded on being thrown overboard. We made a signal that in future they were not to be ditched in the anchorage, an unpleasant and unhealthy habit.' A little complacency had perhaps begun to set in, on the beaches and across the anchorage, and on *Belfast*, although this was doubtless dispelled by the arrival of the wounded.

As the Allied armies enlarged the beachhead and hospitals began to be established ashore, the need to bring wounded soldiers out to the warships lessened, but certainly a steady flow continued for the first few days of the landings. Bob Shrimpton recalled German as well as Allied casualties aboard:

Of course we had boats coming back to the ship with injured aboard, not only British soldiers but German soldiers as well. They were treated before being put aboard destroyers and taken off out. [I remember] having young Germans sitting in our mess decks, being fed cups of tea and cigarettes, and thinking that could have been me. A lot of them had been injured on the beaches, and they were saying 'big guns big guns boom'. They were most impressed by the gunnery of the naval forces.

Interestingly, no other veterans refer to prisoners being held on board, and neither does the ship's log.

Belfast's guns were in action almost constantly throughout 8 June, until well into the evening. At one point the ship was called upon to assist its own FOB, who according to Peter Brooke Smith was apparently being 'molested' by a German battery hidden in a wood. This was, perhaps,

Left: 'Evidently sappers ashore had given the Royal Marines some German land mines to ditch and they had exploded on being thrown overboard. We made a signal that in future they were not to be ditched in the anchorage, an unpleasant and unhealthy habit.' – Peter Brooke Smith.
A very posed photograph of a group of Londoners, Royal Navy Commandos of the Landing Craft Obstacle Clearance Units, on the beach at La Rivière.

an incident recalled by Bob Shrimpton:

> Suddenly a target would come up, the spotters ashore would have a target for us to fire at and ... they would direct the fire from ashore, and we would perhaps fire for ten minutes or quarter of an hour and then stop and then wait for another target to come up. I remember one incident, there were some German guns that were hidden in a wood and we fired on the wood to knock these guns out.

With no serious submarine threat, and a multitude of specialist anti-submarine ships deployed to protect the anchorage, Shrimpton had been released from his duties as ASDIC operator, and was instead a lookout on the Bridge, from where he had a perfect view of what followed. When *Belfast's* fall of shot became lost in the trees, the frustrated FOB apparently called for a rather blunter instrument to deal with the troublesome battery:

> They called in one of these American rocket-firing landing craft and I've never seen anything like it. It just was motionless in the water and it began firing these rockets and it fired literally hundreds of them and ... the landing craft was just enveloped in a pall of smoke as these rockets were going off and they just set this wood afire from end to end.

It is interesting that most veterans invariably attribute the invention of any unusual or clever technology to 'the Americans': the rocket-firing LCTs were in fact British-designed!

The night of 8/9 June was once again badly broken, adding to the exhaustion of *Belfast's* crew. As well as the relentless booming of the battleship HMS *Rodney's* 16-inch guns between 03:00 and 05:00, the ship's log reveals a litany of alarms, a reasonably typical night for Normandy in early June 1944:

00:25 Plane shot down over beaches
00:35 Warning E-boats NNE of Sword

Above: Prisoners jammed into an LCT near Le Hamel, awaiting transport back to Britain. In the background is LCT 886 which was heavily damaged on D-Day. Many of these 'German' soldiers are reluctant conscripts from Poland and Ukraine, known as *Osttruppen*. Given the choice between serving their erstwhile enemy or death in a German POW camp, nearly half a million eastern Europeans joined the *Wehrmacht,* which sent them west rather than risk them deserting to rejoin the Red Army.

00:10 – 00:20 Bombs dropped at intervals and flak, and searchlights put up by British troops

03:10 Enemy destroyers approaching A3 area from NW

03:18 Enemy destroyers a/c 350° Brg 065° from *Belfast*

03:25 Enemy destroyers turn back towards area Sword defence line. [*Belfast*] illuminates area with starshell

05:18 Enemy bomber attacked harbour, dropped one stick of bombs in the sea. Action Stations

05:40 Fall out from Action Stations. 6" remain closed up for bombardment. (Log 1)

Peter Brooke Smith noted that five enemy aircraft were shot down during the night of 8/9 June. Night-time was when *Belfast*'s secondary guns came into their own. Although notionally dual purpose, the cruiser's six twin 4-inch Mark XVI* high-angle gun mounts were most useful as anti-aircraft guns. When many of the ship's company were trying to snatch some much-needed sleep, therefore, men like Denis Watkinson were preparing for action. Watkinson was part of a ten-man 4-inch gun crew: 'You had a layer, a trainer, the shell-setter, the Captain of the Gun and you also had a Petty Officer on the side of the gun, and then you had the loaders.' He spent most nights closed-up at action stations on the upper deck, wrapped in his asbestos anti-flash gear, half-blinded by gun flash and deafened by the high-velocity crack of the guns: 'When them two guns went off ... the flash used to come back and them two guns going off together, and you had nothing in your ears.' Watkinson was a trainer, and generally, if the 4-inch guns were firing under director control, his job was simply to watch a pair of pointers and shout as soon as they were lined up: 'You shove it up the spout, and there's a captain of the gun standing there and the other ones putting it up the other one, and then when I was trainer I used to have to shout 'trainer on' ... then they would fire.'

For Watkinson and his 'oppos' (mates), the night was 'the worst time', fighting a battle of which most of the crew were entirely unaware. Certainly he would have violently disagreed with Charles Simpson's blasé assessment that 'We had thousands of aircraft of every kind but very rarely any enemy aircraft. We had never to open fire on enemy aircraft'.

Fear was a luxury for which they simply did not have time. Watkinson recalled:

You're so busy doing what you've got to do, you seem to block any feelings out. While you're doing this, you're not thinking 'I hope I don't get it, I hope this, I hope that'! You don't do that, you get on with it and you take it ... It's very hard to describe ... It doesn't feel like anything, it just feels that you've got to do this and you hope you're doing it right ...There's something in the nature of people which blocks that out.

With every ship in the anchorage firing, it was almost impossible for an individual crew to tell whether they had hit anything, although Watkinson was sure his crew scored at least one success, probably one of the five enemy aircraft Peter Brooke Smith noted as having been shot down during the night of 8/9 June:

We were firing nearly every night ... we did manage to get one once [when] I was on lookout. We were stood down at the time on the gun, and I had to

Below: 'We had thousands of aircraft of every kind.' – Charles Simpson. Naval gunnery was not the only source of overwhelming Allied firepower in Normandy. By day, Allied fighter bombers roamed unopposed over the battlefield, making it almost impossible for German vehicles to move. This photograph shows the aftermath of an attack by RAF Typhoons of No. 121 Wing on German armour near Coutances, on 29 July 1944. The graves of some of the occupants can be seen on the left.

go on lookout, we took it in turns, and this German had been hit ... he was on fire and he was circling round and round and he was getting lower and lower all the time and I thought 'Good God, I hope he gets down before he gets to us 'cos he'll hit us'.

Fortunately for *Belfast*, the German aircraft slammed into the sea some distance away. The next morning Watkinson thought he spotted the bodies of the downed airmen in the water: 'You can tell they're airmen 'cos they have leather jackets on you know.' And so, after another sleep-deprived night, another wearying day on the gunline began – 9 June 1944. If we imagine D-Day as a 'naval battle' at all, most of us perhaps assume that the real danger for sailors ended on 6 June, and thenceforth the Battle of Normandy became a purely land battle, with only soldiers and airmen risking their lives. This assumption could not be further from the truth. The Allied navies remained at the sharp end of a very real, very dangerous battle for control of the invasion beachhead throughout June and well into early July. Just because hindsight tells us that very few ships were lost and that German air and sea power was a shadow of its former self, we should not assume that the men on the thousands of ships anchored and exposed in the confined waters of the Baie-de-la-Seine shared this rosy view. Knowing he died on one of the few ships to be sunk would have been small comfort to a sailor expiring in the cold, oil-polluted waters off the Normandy coast. Constant 'tip and run' bombing raids, and other new threats which unfolded over the coming weeks, had a corrosive, sapping effect on men's morale and energy.

By the end of three days on the gunline, stuffed into an almost airless compartment, processing an endless stream of morse code messages as they beeped hypnotically into their headsets and transcribing them at a relentless 25 words per minute, the teenage Wireless Operator Len Beardsley and his 'oppos' were exhausted. First to go was the young rating alongside him:

We were doing four hours on and four hours off all the time we were down there and after a while you got very sleepy. This poor young fella, he was next to me. He was on a different frequency ... taking messages from some other department and he nodded off. The Petty Officer of the watch came around and looked at him and said 'You're asleep aren't you?' 'Oh, oh, er, oh not me!' and he said 'yes you were and I'm going to report you, asleep in the face of the enemy'.

The Petty Officer put the young rating on a charge, and he was brought before Captain Parham, who with typical empathy understood the pressures he had been under and dismissed it. Len Beardsley rightly realised that 'I could have nodded off myself quite easily and missed the message and then I would have been "Len in the cart"'. Shortly afterwards it was his turn:

All the time it was constant ... 24 hours [on] the admiralty transmitter ... there was just me ... Each message is numbered, you see, and if you missed a number then the benches would say 'where's message 86?' ... I missed one but they didn't come back to me. They accepted that I'd missed and they said 'Oh all right Sparks' ... I fell asleep! But I didn't know that I'd fallen asleep, all I knew was I'd missed the message. I couldn't understand it, I thought well I must have dozed off. Four hours on four hours off, 24 hours a day, I mean crikey! After a while you just ... I didn't know.

Fortunately, the more practical commanding officers had developed an informal system for dealing with the vagaries of exhausted operators – they simply signalled the nearest ship with a lamp and asked for the content of the missing signal. That way, regulations were satisfied without the need to punish very tired, very young sailors. Beardsley continued: 'No doubt the other ships ... would signal us and say have you got message 34 because we seem to have missed it! It was all everybody helping everybody else.'

This monotonous work was doubtless made more tiring by the fact that the operators themselves had no idea what they were processing; the signals could have been literally anything:

I couldn't read the code ... I left that to all the people on the desk to break down what the codes meant ... I never knew what was in any of them! Most of it was not anything much to do with the *Belfast*, really, it was for the fleet. All the fleet messages, and you had to read every one just in case there was a message for you!

At the end of a shift, Beardsley and his oppos ate, and then just collapsed:

The first thing you did was grab something to eat and then catch up on your sleep. You used to get your head down and then ... your chums used to wake you and say 'come on you're on duty in ten minutes, up and out', and off you used to go ... You were so tired and sleepy, you used to just drop off. I didn't have any difficulty in falling to sleep at all … if you were lying down in the corridor asleep they just used to step over.

Life on the gunline was not just hard on the men, the relentless bombarding was hard on *Belfast* herself as well, as Bert Brown recalled:

> The vibration was heavy. In fact if you look at the *Belfast* now you'll see that the wiring is fastened to the bulkheads by studs and brackets, and there's nuts on it and it's screwed up tight and the wiring is just lined along the bulkhead. By the time we were finished in July, the vibration had caused a lot of those studs to snap off and the wiring was hanging in loops in places. [And] the light bulbs … when the guns fired, on the mess decks below it would shake out half of the light bulbs and they'd just shake out of the sockets and break on the deck. They were always replacing light bulbs when the guns were firing.

The morning of 9 June was quiet, once the Royal Engineers ashore had finished carrying out 'counter mining' – a military euphemism for blowing up enemy explosives – but the afternoon brought a flurry of activity off the beachhead. The first of a new wave of Corncob blockships was towed into place just before midday and scuttled in position shortly afterwards. Sailors like Bob Shrimpton were amazed at the ingenuity, as they watched the Mulberry harbour gradually evolve in the weeks after D-Day. Years later, his enthusiasm for Allied ingenuity was still apparent:

Below: 'A sheltered spot for supply ships to go in.' – Bob Shrimpton. Supply ships high and dry at low water inside the Mulberry harbour at Arromanches. Two Ducks are driving across the beach, which has been entirely cleared of obstacles. The outer breakwater and blockships can be seen in the background.

It was an amazing sight. And the thinking of how they built not only the Mulberry harbour but where they put those old ships ... they'd brought down from Southampton. And they sunk them in a half-circle just outside Arromanches, and so that gave a sheltered spot for supply ships to go in. It was really brilliant the way they did that.

At 13:55 the three Royal Marines who had survived the landing craft explosion of the day before were transferred ashore, and shortly afterwards *Belfast* began the afternoon's bombardment work, targeting a pair of enemy strong points located well over ten miles inland. After 15 minutes of firing, both were reported in the log to have been hit. By this time, *Belfast* had a new consort. Like the rocket ships, it was another unusual craft which many of the veterans remembered well: the 15-inch gunned monitor HMS *Roberts*, which was reported as closing in alongside *Belfast* at 15:45. Len Beardsley was impressed, remembering that when *Roberts* fired her guns 'they used to shake us ... by golly you knew about it if you heard them'. Bob Shrimpton was particularly taken by her:

Then there was another amazing boat that was there ... it was an old 16-inch gun [sic] monitor ... and it only had six foot draught, and it would sail in as close as possible and the twin barrelled 16-inch guns would fire these shells, and the force of the shells going out propelled the boat backwards and it would come hurtling back and then it would have to steam up on to the beach again.

Monitors were developed during the First World War to provide gunfire support to troops ashore. Generally they were distinguished by both their shallow draught, which allowed them to get close inshore, and their disproportionately heavy armament for a relatively small ship. Their name derives from John Ericsson's revolutionary USS *Monitor*, the first warship to carry a revolving gun turret, but the monitors of the First and Second World Wars were developed for an entirely different purpose. Understandably many of the watching sailors believed *Roberts* was an 'old' ship, but in fact she had not been built until after the start of the war. One of her 15-inch guns can be seen today outside IWM London.

With the fighting moving further inland and much of the immediate threat from German shore batteries neutralised, the anchorage was now deemed to be safe for the larger, more vulnerable transport ships which were bringing in subsequent waves of troops. As they started to arrive,

the Baie-de-la-Seine became, in Peter Brooke Smith's words, 'a maze of shipping'. 'The ocean was just one mass, it was like Hyde Park Corner', Bob Shrimpton remembered years later, 'they all had to maintain their station, every ship had to know what station and what target it was facing, that's the important thing. We kept on moving around because the 88mm guns could really pick you off from a great distance so we kept up a little backwards and forwards cruising movement'.

This was a strange situation for Charles Simpson and his engine room team, who fundamentally had very little to do, but nevertheless had to remain at their posts and be prepared to move the ship at a moment's notice if required, or respond to any unexpected emergency:

> We gained information from the Commander (E) that it was unlikely we would be called upon to move the ship for several hours, but we would of course have to be at action stations against enemy fire, against damage to the ship, fire breaking out, compartments flooded. We would still have been an [enemy] objective. We could have been fired upon by guns ashore or bombed from above. It was considered that the engine room should remain at a reduced state of readiness ... We were kept at half an hour's notice for the first few days ... After some time ... we were ordered to move.

It was considered necessary for us to go to another part of the landing area to bombard objectives in that place, so engine rooms were called to action and we then proceeded as would have done in peacetime from ... Juno beach to Gold beach or vice versa.

As the afternoon faded into evening, the by now familiar air raids began, the first recorded alert being at 17:10 when 12 Messerschmitt 109 fighter bombers dropped bombs inland. Friendly fire was still an issue, an interesting testimony to the enduring menace posed by German air power – had the Luftwaffe not been a threat, nervous naval gunners would not have still been inclined to shoot at anything that flew. One miscreant was Peter Brooke Smith's friend and fellow RNVR Temporary Lieutenant Tony Woodall, who managed to 'fire two salvoes at a Typhoon in mistake for a Focke-Wulf 190'. Brooke Smith amusingly noted that 'at least he can now say he has fired his guns in the 2nd Front!'

Sometimes, the anti-aircraft defence of the anchorage was co-ordinated into what was known as an 'umbrella barrage', concentrating a limited

Above: '22:30 Action Stations ... Magnificent display of flak – best yet. Parabolas of red tracer, some self-destructive and bursting in bright sparkles, one after another, at the end of their curve.'
– Peter Brooke Smith. Photographed from the cruiser HMS *Mauritius,* tracer fire from warships streaks the darkness as an almost impenetrable screen is put up against enemy bombers, during a night raid on the anchorage at Ouistreham off Normandy.

burst of fire on a predetermined elevation and bearing to deter an incoming enemy air raid by forming an impenetrable wall or 'umbrella' of bursting shells. For some of the anti-aircraft gunners, like David Jones, the umbrella barrage was just another mystery which was his responsibility to help make happen, not understand: '"Umbrella umbrella umbrella!!" they used to shout and ... the guns used to go on some fixed bearings and elevations and fire half a dozen shots. I think it was some kind of barrage but we never really knew.'

Night-time intruder raids by just a few enemy aircraft triggered the most overwhelming response, as every ship in the anchorage opened up, supported by army gunners ashore. Peter Brooke Smith described the scene on the night of 9/10 June: '22:30 Action Stations ... Magnificent display of flak – best yet. Parabolas of red tracer, some self-destructive and bursting in bright sparkles, one after another, at the end of their curve. Sticks of bombs dropped – rapid spotches of fire – followed by a huge blaze in the direction of Courseulles. Phosphorous incendiaries or markers also showered down.'

On other occasions the gunners fired strips of aluminium foil known as 'window', to baffle enemy radar, instead of high explosives. Radio-controlled glider bombs, which had been used with devastating effect against the Allied invasion fleets at Anzio and Salerno, were another fear. By June 1944, however, Allied scientists had identified the radio frequency used by the controlling radio sets and the warships were able to jam it. The code for operating this jamming equipment was Tiptree Vermin, and it appears in *Belfast*'s log with monotonous regularity during those June nights – although, as it turned out, no glider bombs were used against the Operation 'Neptune' armada.

Later in the night of 9/10 June, *Belfast* was again disturbed by gunfire, as the outer screen of destroyers and light craft, known as the Trout Line, drove off an E-boat attack. Finally, to kill off sleep once and for all, the cruiser was ordered to carry out a rare night-time shoot, against a formation of German tanks in a wood. The bombardment was successful and the 'buzz' soon spread through the lower deck that *Belfast* had destroyed first an armoured brigade, then an entire *panzer* division.

Above: 'They were held up by a panzer division ... within half an hour I don't think there were any tanks left.' – Bob Shrimpton. A German *Panzerkampfwagen VI* Tiger I tank overturned during the Normandy campaign, either by Allied heavy bombing or naval gunfire. This type of vehicle weighed 60 tons.

Whatever the truth of it, there was no doubt that the soldiers ashore greatly appreciated *Belfast*'s intervention. Bob Shrimpton explains:

> Well we had several signals back ... from the army spotters praising the gunnery because they said it was so accurate ... just before Caen they were held up by a panzer division, they were in a forest and they required bombardment and I think within half an hour I don't think there were any tanks left. They had army spotters out, they would spot close to the target. You'd fire a couple of sighting rounds and they would tell you to shift target or raise your elevation. But the army officers did send back recorded messages saying 'brilliant gunfire, brilliant', so that's quite a tribute to the gunnery officers.

There is no doubt that the awesome power of naval gunfire, coupled with the Allies' overwhelming air superiority, made the Battle of Normandy virtually unwinnable for the Germans; it was simply impossible for them to put together a co-ordinated counterattack or to move armoured vehicles around by day or by night without attracting a devastating response. It was not unheard of for naval gunfire to overturn a 60-ton Tiger tank. One German soldier, serving with the 12th SS Panzer Division *Hitlerjugend*, described stumbling across the devastating aftermath of one such bombardment: 'Here we encountered the most terrible images of the war. The enemy had virtually cut to pieces units of the Panzer Lehr Division with heavy weapons. SPWs [armoured halftracks] and equipment had been ripped apart; next to them on the ground, and even hanging in the trees, were body parts of dead comrades. A terrible silence covered all.'

Peter Brooke Smith finally got to sleep at 04:00. An hour later he was up again for dawn action stations. At 05:30 he turned in again, so exhausted that he overslept, missed breakfast, and was late relieving his opposite number on watch.

Saturday 10 June began with waves of Marauder and Flying Fortress bombers sweeping majestically inland, followed a couple of hours later by the welcome sight of Spitfires landing and taking off from one of the newly constructed temporary airstrips behind the beaches, and endless streams of troops and vehicles pouring into the beachhead. Although the relentless work of bombardment continued throughout the day, there was no doubt aboard that the tide was turning – after a few days of uncertainty when nothing much seemed to be progressing, as Bob Shrimpton recalled: 'I think the first initial object was that the men had been pouring ashore all day and we were now getting heavy equipment ashore. Then there was a lull after about three or four days ... because nobody was moving forward ... and there was just that little bit of a worry that we might have to bring them all back out again.'

Certainly the atmosphere aboard was more relaxed, and at 11:30 Admiral Dalrymple-Hamilton, his secretary, and *Belfast*'s Royal Marine Captain, G C Belbin, went ashore in the ship's motor boat, apparently for some sightseeing. They did not return until 15:40, bringing with them gifts and plenty of 'sea stories', according to Peter Brooke Smith: 'There were Normandy roses on the Wardroom table today after the Admiral's Secretary, Major and the mad Bolitho returned from a visit ashore with the Admiral. Graphic descriptions of what they had seen, including the anti-landing craft obstructions, some with old percussion capped shells lashed to the top.'

By the time Brooke Smith found the roses, *Belfast* was on her way home. Perhaps fortunately for the ship and the very weary men aboard, the day's firing had finally exhausted the cruiser's ammunition supply, and at 20:00 she weighed anchor and headed back to Portsmouth to take on more. As *Belfast* crossed the channel, all around they could see the evidence of Allied power: endless columns of laden ships heading to the beachhead, and similar convoys of empty LCTs and the iconic, mass-produced American freighters known as Liberty Ships returning to the UK to collect yet more men, equipment and supplies. After years on the defensive, some of the watching sailors simply could not take in the extent of the power at the disposal of the Allies. Bob Shrimpton was one who 'couldn't make out where it's all been hidden. Why didn't anybody notice these sort of things? ... Where did they come from and how long had they hidden them there?'

Finally, at four minutes past midnight on Sunday 11 June 1944 – after more than a week at sea, much of it at action stations and under enemy gunfire and air attack – *Belfast* dropped her anchor, just under a mile off Stokes Bay Pier,

Below: 'There were Normandy roses on the Wardroom table today after the Admiral's Secretary ... returned from a visit ashore.' – Peter Brooke Smith. Three ratings from a Royal Navy minesweeper enjoying a carefully staged 'run ashore' in Normandy. According to the original caption the Naval Chaplain in Arromanches arranged wholesome, media-friendly *'rambles, sports and picnics'* – one can perhaps imagine their views! Left to right they are Telegraphist E F Guyatt, Signalman E V Hammond, and Wireman V J Howe.

near the ammunition depots which lined the Gosport side of Portsmouth harbour. At ten past midnight, the log reports: 'finished with main engines' (Log 1). *Belfast* was home, for a while, and her ship's company had a welcome break from the noise and strain of the gunline. In fact the break was rather longer than anticipated, as the ammunition lighters which were supposed to arrive at 01:00 were late, according to rumour because their civilian crews were unwilling to work at night – 'If so, they should be shot!', noted the uncompromising Peter Brooke Smith in his diary. There is of course no evidence for this allegation, which may well have simply been a reflection of the well-known antipathy between the RN and the dockyard 'maties'.

It was not until 06:15 the following morning, as recorded in the log, that three ammunition lighters were finally lashed to the cruiser's port side and the elderly Royal Fleet Auxiliary oiler *Kimmerol* to the starboard. The back-breaking work of loading ammunition and stores was delegated to personnel from Portsmouth Naval Base, leaving *Belfast's* ship's company free to rest. Peter Brooke Smith slept through the entire controversy over the lighters, and when he finally woke on the morning of 11 June he found himself somewhat disorientated:

> When I woke I expected to be back off Normandy, with ammunitioning completed according to programme. Opened my scuttle very cautiously in case of blast should our guns fire, and looked out. Yes! There was the same little town with the spires; there were the wood, beaches, landing craft and barrage balloons. It was not till I went down to breakfast and looked out of the Wardroom ports that I saw we were off Lee on Solent, and what I had been looking at on the other side was Ryde, Isle of Wight.

It is a measure of the continuing importance of naval gunfire support to the success of the Battle for Normandy that *Belfast's* replenishment was turned around so quickly. By 14:25 the ship had weighed anchor, and was on her way back across the Channel. With such a short break, there was no opportunity for leave or even a run ashore, although there was a welcome delivery of mail. This was less welcome for Peter Brooke Smith, however, who learned that his brother Ted, who was in the army, had been seriously wounded in Italy. For many, it was also their first opportunity to read Rex North's purple prose in the *Sunday Pictorial*, described by Brooke Smith as 'unmitigated rot'!

The journey back was largely uneventful, although the log records some drastic avoiding action to prevent a collision with a corvette at 16:23 – a reflection, perhaps, of the congested waters and the tiredness of both crews. By 18:55, *Belfast* was anchored once again in the now-familiar waters off Ver-sur-Mer and Courseulles, the Officer of the Watch recording in the log once again the steady litany of aircraft sightings and warnings of enemy warships. The night was less disturbed than usual, although still broken by 'two noticeably loud explosions' at 01:10, plus searchlights, starshells and a sudden eruption of anti-aircraft fire (Log 1).

Belfast returned to the gunline on Monday 12 June. The morning began quietly enough, with a reassuringly vast formation of B17 Flying Fortress and B24 Liberator bombers passing over to the south at 08:30, returning an hour later. In a stark reminder that the airmen's war was no 'picnic' either, even at this late stage in the war, as the aircraft passed over *Belfast* one started to slowly descend, obviously in difficulties, and eight parachutes blossomed in a line behind it. Later in the morning, at 11:35, the Officer of the Watch recorded the arrival of the destroyer HMS *Kelvin*, carrying some VIPs. Six days after D-Day, Winston Churchill had finally got his way and was visiting the beaches, accompanied by the Chief of the Imperial General Staff, Field Marshal Sir Alan Brooke, and the veteran South African soldier and statesman Field Marshal Jan Smuts (as noted by both Brook Smith and *Belfast*'s log). An hour and a half later, Churchill, Smuts and Brooke passed serenely across *Belfast*'s stern, making for the shore, as a photoreconnaissance Mosquito passed up and down the beaches, photographing the occasion with a strong escort of Spitfires.

Of all the days for a stark reminder that Normandy was still a very dangerous place, therefore, 12 June 1944 was probably the worst. One well-placed bomb could have changed the course of the war. An hour and half after the prime minister had landed, four German pilots were presented with a career-defining opportunity, albeit one of which they were entirely unaware. Aboard the warships there is no doubt that a sense of complacency had by now definitely set in, at least as far as daylight air attacks were concerned. Len Beardsley was one of several sailors who were just a little too relaxed:

> We came back and re-ammoed after three days ... and then went straight back to D-Day and started: 'bang, bang bang' again! After that the landing was successful and everything went more or less peaceful after that. It was a warm sunny summer's day up on top, and we changed from four on four

Above: 'Kelvin approaching anchorage. Prime Minister, Field Marshal Smuts
and Sir Alan Brooke aboard.' — *Belfast*'s log, 12 June 1944.
Winston Churchill with Field Marshal Jan Smuts, of the Imperial War Cabinet (right),
and Field Marshal Sir Alan Brooke, CIGS (Chief of the Imperial General Staff),
on the bridge of the destroyer HMS *Kelvin*.

off to the usual ... four on and eight off and I thought 'thank God for that'! So I used to then go up on the upper deck in the lovely sunshine and I used to flake out up there ... we were still down off the Normandy beaches, but everything was very peaceful and very quiet then.

Charles Bunbury was also daydreaming, as he recorded in his journal: 'We were caught napping one afternoon, on Monday 12 June ... the flight deck was covered with men sunbathing and all the guns' crews were taking it easy too ... suddenly three FW190s swooped down and dropped six bombs off the bow of the ship, only about 200 yards from us.' Peter Brooke Smith also witnessed the attack: 'About 14:45 hours three explosions shook the ship. Five [sic] FW190s had dived down from 5000 feet and straddled us. Not a shot fired. Action Stations sounded, "shutting the stable door" as Young said as he passed me on way to our stations!'

The incident was over in seconds, and few of the *Belfast* men were aware of how dangerous it might have been; perhaps if more of them had served off Crete in 1941, during the heyday of the Luftwaffe's fearsome ability to hit and sink warships, they might have been less blasé. Brian Butler summed up the incident pithily, remembering that 'it was a very fast plane... we all ducked!' Denis Watkinson was lazing on the Pom Pom deck, ironically surrounded by eight-barrelled anti-aircraft guns, chatting to an Australian friend: 'All I could hear was this scream ... and the machine guns and the scream of the bombs. I just fell flat on the floor 'cos there was no warning! But all the bombs fell around us, we were very very lucky again.'

As the Focke-Wulfs screamed away, their pilots desperately trying to regain altitude and make themselves scarce before the RAF arrived to take revenge, David Jones noticed that at least one of them had left a reminder of his visit: 'About ... two or three feet above the gun was a boat and the chocks that hold the boat in, there was a 20mm cannon shell had hit that and hadn't exploded. It was buried in there about three feet above our heads. It was only a 20mm cannon shell but even so if it had gone off!' Peter Brooke Smith wrote later that 'X Turret opened up at nearest enemy

airfield and straddled it!' The payback was belated, but with the optimism of youth Charles Bunbury still wrote hopefully that 'we might even have caught the FW190s landing there'.

The air war over the gunline was still lively, particularly in the evening and after dark. Recorded in the log, at 16:10 an unidentified aircraft was shot down near *Belfast*; ominously, an 'object' – almost certainly an airman – fell from it but 'no parachute opened'. Later on, an over-enthusiastic gunner aboard a neighbouring ship astern of *Belfast* shot a neat line of 20mm holes through her hangar, and the watchkeepers on the cruiser's bridge observed a formation of Allied Boston bombers fly into heavy anti-aircraft fire. One aircraft was hit. Peter Brooke Smith noted six parachutes safely emerge, after which the doomed bomber apparently flew in circles for 20 minutes with no-one at the controls before crashing in flames behind the little town of St Aubin. 'This Second Front is very good for aircraft recognition', Brooke Smith wryly noted, 'Have seen Spits, Thunderbolts, Mustangs, Typhoons, Dakotas, Mitchells, Bostons, Liberators, Lightnings, Forts – even a Walrus'. Later, the log recorded the now familiar E-boat alarms, searchlights, flak, the inevitable ominous Tiptree Vermin notes, and at 03:37 a vicious little skirmish between light coastal forces craft (Log 1).

On the morning of 14 June, *Belfast* moved to Arromanches, where the British Mulberry harbour was growing rapidly, to the fascination of

Above: 'A colossal port!' – Peter Brooke Smith.
The full extent of Mulberry B at Arromanches, with its blockships and breakwaters, piers, pontoons and roadways, shown in a stitched together montage of aerial photographs. Hundreds of ships and smaller craft can be seen sheltering inside it.

the watching sailors. 'I remember the Mulberry harbour', Ron Jesse said decades later, 'the Mulberry Harbour was first of all a set of sunken ships which formed a breakwater and then it was a more sophisticated device made out of concrete moles'. Peter Brooke Smith called it 'a colossal port' by now, and counted 20 sunken merchant ships in the breakwater, along with the old French battleship *Courbet*, the Royal Navy cruiser *Durban* and the Dutch cruiser *Sumatra*.

By now *Belfast's* men were starting to find bombardment operations off Normandy almost monotonous. 'It became routine', Ron Jesse remembered almost guiltily, 'that's a terrible thing to say but it became routine. "We shall be firing in five minutes time" and bang-bang, bang-bang, and you got on with what you were doing without paying attention to it'. Certainly any sense of concern or uncertainty about the ultimate success of the invasion seemed to have evaporated for many. By now the ship was operating entirely at the disposal of the army observers ashore, sometimes under the direction of a spotter aircraft. Ron Jesse continued:

> We were then put on to ranging further inland, and for the next six weeks we went further and further inland ...There were men assigned with radio connections to spot our fall of shot ... It's so accurate for a ship, which is capable of shooting at a moving target when it's moving itself, so accurate when it is standing still and shooting at another ... stationary target. We were full of confidence. We couldn't help feeling sorry for the blighters.

The anchorage was still extraordinarily busy, eight days after the invasion. 'You couldn't look without you saw a ship, it was absolutely black with ships', Jesse vividly recalled:

> Destroyers, battleships further off out booming away, cargo ships unloading their cargo ... but we were walking around the ship just as if we were on holiday, really, when we weren't on duty. I saw the Captain once standing on top of one of the high parts with a pair of binoculars trying to identify a gun on the shore that he wished he could know where to shoot it.

'It was', he concluded, 'all very casual and confident'.

Only the out of the ordinary was worth recalling. Brian Butler remembered a particularly unusual shot: 'I remember one small thing. There was a church in the town there and ... we'd fired a shell and it went straight through the church spire and ... it didn't explode, it went

on to its target and there was a hole right through the church spire!
You could see the light right through the church spire.' Gordon Painter
remembered the shot through the church spire as well, and even years
later the recollection made him oddly uncomfortable. The received
wisdom aboard was that the Germans were using the building as an
ammunition store but even so, for Painter it was:

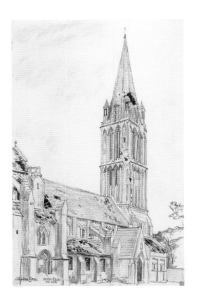

> nothing to be proud of I think. When you have to fight for your country,
> you just have to do your job and you have to do as you're told. Those guys
> were human beings the same as we were ... It did really sink into you exactly
> what it was all about ... but that's war. And we were doing it for freedom
> and everything that this country deserves and the future of this country.

By the evening of 14 June *Belfast* had run out of ammunition once
more, after just two days of firing. (This might indicate that the late

Far left: 'We'd fired a shell and it went straight through the church spire!' – Brian Butler. Pencil drawing of the badly damaged church at Bernières-sur-Mer, by war artist Stephen Bone. According to Bone's original title, the steeple was shelled after German snipers started to use it. It is not clear whether this is the church to which Butler refers.

Bottom left: 'It was a continuous thing … the ship was sort of like field artillery' – Robert Brown. Royal Marines aboard HMS *Sirius* proudly show off more than 2,000 5.25-inch (133mm) shell cases, each one fired off by the cruiser's X Turret, trained outboard behind them. X Turret was always traditionally manned by Royal Marines in Royal Navy warships. Like many of the bombarding warships, *Sirius* had spent most of the war in the Mediterranean, where she returned in August 1944.

Left: Liberation! A group of French school children play in a pool on the beach at Arromanches. In the background, a small coaster sits high and dry on the sand, apparently preparing to discharge its cargo into a cluster of American-built GMC 2½ ton 'deuce and a half' cargo trucks. The surrounding soldiers do not appear to be in any hurry to start!

arrival of the ammunition lighters the last time she was at Portsmouth meant that the magazines and shell rooms had not been fully replenished.) At first, the 'buzz' that swept through the ship as she steamed through the night, once again passing endless serried lines of Liberty Ships, LSTs and other merchant ships and transports, was that *Belfast* was returning to Scapa Flow – prompting, according to Brook Smith, 'great indignation onboard'. Whatever her ultimate destination, however, her first stop was once again Portsmouth. *Belfast* dropped anchor off Spithead at 19:53, with the inevitable oiler alongside a couple of hours later.

For a few days, at least, the war was on hold.

CHAPTER SIX
LAST DAYS

'We used to listen into the German wireless telephoning, between the motor torpedo boats ... and we actually heard ... one chap telling another in German exactly where the *Belfast* was by name.' — *Captain Frederick Parham*

This time the ship's respite was longer. Once again, ratings for the base were drafted in to re-ammunition and store the ship, so for the *Belfast* men log entries contain more references to the magical word, 'liberty'. It began almost immediately – the first boatload of matelots was away less than an hour after the anchor splashed into the Solent. Peter Brooke Smith was 'swamped' with requests for night leave in Portsmouth, although he preferred to get out of his uniform for only the second time since 6 June and, like many of his shipmates, sleep. The contrast between the frenetic log entries from the gunline and the infrequent, sedate notes from Portsmouth is stark. Nothing happened worth recording apart from the occasional arrival and departure of ships: *Onslow*, *Saumarez*, *Middleton*, *Mauritius*. Doubtless the *Belfast* men were glad of the peace, although presumably the visit by a group of VAD (Voluntary Aid Detachment) nurses for half an hour at the end of the 15 June was a welcome distraction. One can only speculate about the purpose – Pink Gins in the Wardroom perhaps?

Although there was no time for long leave, some of the local men were allowed to return home and visit their families. Lieutenant-Commander J A Meares, *Belfast*'s Navigating Officer, was an Isle of Wight man, and he managed to arrange for a group of six island men to spend a welcome night at home, even though the Isle of Wight was a restricted area. Brian Butler got back to Ryde, although 'with the strict instructions that we had to be on the end of Ryde Pier at half past seven in the morning and woe betide us if we weren't there because the ship was sailing at noon!' The gesture did not endear Butler and the others to their oppos: 'We were very lucky we were able to get [home] and the rest of the ship's company weren't well pleased about that.' The log carefully records that 'Isle of Wight native libertymen' returned safely aboard at 07:35 on 16 June (Log 1).

David Jones was another man who managed to get home. Although he was brought up in Kirby, by now his parents were running a pub in Southampton. The 18-year-old was threatened with terrifying consequences if he over-indulged in their hospitality: 'They said if you don't turn up in the morning you'll be charged with desertion in the face of the enemy ... the punishment for which is death! I made sure I got back all right, although it didn't help that the train was late.' The visit was a little surreal. 'Hello Dave, where you been? D-Day?', he was asked. 'What do you mean D-Day?' replied Jones. 'Well you know, second front?' Jones was still bemused: 'What do you mean second front?' His frustrated relatives tried again, 'well you know, invasion of France?' Finally the

Left: A witness to the ferocity of the Royal Navy's war off the Normandy beaches, LCT 608 was attacked by German E-boats on the night of 7/8 June. Although her bow was smashed, the ship's commanding officer, Lieutenant E C Mason RNVR, and his crew managed to bring her back to Britain, where she was eventually repaired.

penny dropped: 'Oh yeah that's where I've been! I didn't know it was called D-Day though or second front, that's how much information we got. We didn't even know we were going there. Nobody ever mentioned we were going to invade France in the morning like!'

Denis Watkinson remembered another man whose parents, in contrast to Jones' family, were blissfully unaware of what he had been doing, and actually had some rather disconcerting news for him: 'There was a lad lived ashore near the ship and the skipper let him go ashore as long as he came back within so many hours when they got the ship all filled up again. When he got in his mother said "God what're you' doing here? I've just been listening to the wireless and Lord Haw Haw says he's sunk you!"'

Back on board *Belfast*, Rear-Admiral Dalrymple-Hamilton was delighted to learn that he had been promoted to Vice-Admiral for his work on the Normandy gunline, and celebrated with drinks with some of the ship's junior officers, including Peter Brooke Smith. There was more good news when Dalrymple-Hamilton confirmed that *Belfast* would in fact be returning to Normandy, not heading north to swing miserably at anchor in Scapa Flow. Brooke Smith, another Hampshire man, managed to get ashore after the Admiral's party, spending the day with Nicholson, the Surgeon, at Bedales, a public school just outside Petersfield where he had taught before the war. The contrast with the rigours of the gunline could not have been more pronounced: 'A lovely day', he wrote, 'hot sun and large white woolly clouds floating over the downs'. To an extent Brooke Smith was visiting an idyllic world which was already ceasing to exist:

> Had tea with Geoffrey and Barbara Crump. Met Ken Keast on the cricket pitch in white flannels giving catching practice. Talked to one of my former pupils. Lovely to be back! Brings back all the happiness of those days I had there to see the children and meet old friends on the staff. Ken very keen that I should visit his house next time and meet his wife, Brenda Harman, whom I supervised for School Certificate Exams in June '39.

Later on 15 June, Brooke Smith met up with Rex North, the war correspondent whose purple prose he had lambasted in his diary. North returned to *Belfast* at 10:30 the next day, and the two men seem to have made their peace: 'His main story had gone to the *Daily Mail*', the embarrassed journalist apparently explained, 'and the drivel in the *Sunday Pictorial* was a by-product.'

But even Portsmouth was not exactly calm. As well as all the regular comings and goings of ships, including some old friends from the gunline like the monitor HMS *Roberts,* the log notes several air-raid alerts, which were probably minelaying 'tip and run' attacks or else the flying bombs which were prevalent across the south of England in the summer of 1944.

As sweating sailors from the naval base stuffed *Belfast* full of ammunition and stores, the ship's company continued to relax properly for the first time since the end of May. Peter Brooke Smith recorded another run ashore with Nicholson on 16 June 'to see his former residence in Dockyard – just like a Cathedral Close'. They strolled around the Dockyard, visiting the newly painted HMS *Victory,* before buying strawberries and wandering into Portsmouth to take in a performance of the comic ballet *Coppelia.* He spent Saturday 17 June sunbathing on the gun deck and listening to the records he had purchased a lifetime ago, just before *Belfast* left the Clyde. Normandy could not have seemed further away.

Belfast weighed anchor and returned to the gunline at 09:00 on Saturday 18 June, passing the battleships *Rodney* and *Ramilles* and threading her way through a large convoy as she crossed the Channel. Just over four hours later, after an uneventful crossing, she was back on the gunline. Admiral Vian paid Dalrymple-Hamilton a brief visit at 18:25, perhaps to congratulate him on his promotion. At 21:35, confirming that the beachhead was still very much a battlefield, a large force of Dakota and Stirling aircraft passed overhead, dropping supplies behind the beaches.

The next day it was the weather not the Germans that proved the greater hazard to the invasion. On 19 June, a great storm blew up, destroying the part-constructed American Mulberry harbour at Omaha beach and badly damaging the British one at Arromanches. The decision was taken to recycle surviving components from Omaha at Arromanches, to ensure at least one viable harbour remained. The *Belfast* men were hardly aware of the storm, riding it out in a 11,500 ton cruiser which had already withstood far worse in the Arctic, although some, including Ron Jesse, remembered its aftermath: 'the Mulberry harbour ... was severely damaged by a storm that blew up.

Below: The floating causeway of Mulberry B at Arromanches flexing during the Great Storm. The gale was believed to be the greatest summer storm to hit the Normandy coast for 40 years, with wind speeds ranging from Force 6 to Force 8. Hundreds of small craft were wrecked or damaged, and the weather cost the Allies 140,000 tons of scheduled supplies and ammunition.

It didn't bother us in the *Belfast*, we had two anchors out and that was that, but it was all blown hither and yon and it was a bit of a mess for quite some time until it was restored.' (*Belfast's* displacement had increased from 10,000 tons as built to 11,500 during her reconstruction after the mining of November 1939.)

Belfast had now relocated to the extreme eastern end of Sword beach, where the front line bumped against the River Orne and the land fighting had stalled badly in the approaches to the battered city of Caen. According to Peter Brooke Smith, the German front line was just four miles from *Belfast* on 21 June, when a shore gun hit a merchant ship alongside. According to Captain Parham, this was why *Belfast* remained on station off Normandy long after many of the other warships had left:

> It meant of course that the nights were pretty broken, one didn't get much sleep and during the day it was off and on all the time waiting for calls from the army and trying to make quite sure that they weren't bogus ones from the Germans, which was a little tricky at times. But there we stayed down the eastern end of the bombardment area and that's really I think why we stayed so much longer than anybody else, because the army got held up in front of Caen and therefore the Germans remained within range of our guns for considerably longer than they did further west.

For the crew, it meant back to nights broken by air-raid alarms, E-boat alerts and gunfire, and days punctuated by the relentless booming of the

guns, as the cruiser, now accompanied by HM ships *Arethusa, Sirius, Argonaut* and *Orion,* resumed her relentless work of bombarding.

By now, the night time 'tip and run' raiders had moved on from making largely ineffective bombing raids in the dark to mine laying, a far more serious threat. By June 1944, the Allies had developed effective countermeasures to both German magnetic mines, which responded to distortions to the earth's magnetic field caused by a passing ship, and to acoustic mines, which responded to the noise made by a ship's engines, as well as the more conventional tethered 'contact' varieties. But off the Normandy gunline they introduced a new and far more deadly device. Pressure mines, known as 'oyster' mines, were activated by ships passing above altering the water pressure and triggering the firing device. The Germans laid around 400 in the waters off Normandy. Although the Allies found and dismantled one, according to the Royal Navy's official historian they were 'almost impossible to sweep'. Certainly *Belfast*'s log entries for late June and early July contain countless references to mine sightings, and explosions triggered by nearby ships, although at first most seemed to have escaped serious damage (Log 1). The only effective antidote was to compute the maximum speed at which a ship could move without

Below: HMS *Fury,* herself a victim of both German and natural fury. In action since 1940, the old destroyer struck a mine on 21 June and was then driven ashore in the Great Storm. Although she was refloated and towed back to the UK, she was scrapped in September 1944.

triggering it. This led to a lot of unnerving and very slow manoeuvring, a terrible responsibility for Captain Parham: 'The German aircraft … started laying these things called oyster mines which really were rather a trap because they were touched off simply by the passage of a ship over them … The rule was that when these mines had been laid … we were allowed to proceed on one engine only out of four, going either slow ahead or slow astern.'

Ron Jesse, down in the engine room, also recalled the careful crawling, although he also recalled that by late June, despite these dangers, many of the crew were thoroughly relaxed and confident that it would all be over soon, and would be successful:

A little while afterwards … we were asked to move on one screw only so as not to set off any [mines] that can be set off by the vibration of the water. So we went on one screw at very slow speed along the coast to help bombard Omaha beach … which were having a hard time of it. It was so easy and we were so full of confidence that we relaxed from full action stations and quite often we were up on deck watching what was going on because there was absolutely no response from the enemy.

Jesse was keeping busy, helping the crews of the myriad small craft which tied up alongside *Belfast*, hoping to cadge extra supplies and spares

Left: 'It was all cliffs, you couldn't see anything. [The beach] was narrow … and they were getting slaughtered.' – Denis Watkinson. A survivor from a sunken American landing craft is helped ashore, Omaha Assault Area, 6 June 1944. The defences at Omaha were unexpectedly strong, and very little went as planned on D-Day. Nearly half of all Allied casualties (killed, wounded and missing) on the beaches on 6 June 1944 came at Omaha.

drawn from the big cruiser's well–stocked stores and well-equipped workshops:

> Several small ships came alongside to have repairs done to them and ... if I were off duty and could help with the repairs I did them. I did some in the coppersmiths' shop repairing pipes and things, and I went and jumped down and helped repair them ...They were little small ships, they were tank landing craft, one was an American Coast Guard cutter ... boats really.

The log does not confirm or deny with any clarity whether, as Ron Jesse claimed, *Belfast* actually visited the American sector, but Dennis Watkinson was another veteran who remembered it vividly: 'Later on I remember the Americans, there was landing craft full of black soldiers ... They went past us, well we'd been there from the very beginning [and[they were coming in when it was all cleared ... They were saying "limeys get yourself ashore!" Little did they know what we'd been through! But that's typical American like you know.'

More than half a century afterwards, Watkinson still felt that the US soldiers who had stormed the beaches on 6 June had been given an impossible task:

> When we were firing ... it was all cliffs, you couldn't see anything. [The beach] was narrow ... and they were getting slaughtered ... it must have been terrible for the Americans. I still to this day can't understand what man with any sense would have allowed them to get off that beach and get up there when they could just throw bombs down on them like that, it was terrible.

22 June saw a brief duel with a German battery near Deauville. *Belfast*'s big guns were still in constant action over this period, generally firing two turrets at a time throughout the day, from early in the morning until later at night. Sadly, we do not know on which day one of these shoots generated an unintended consequence which Bernard Thomson recalled with amusement:

Above: 'It must have been terrible for the Americans.' – Denis Watkinson.
The bodies of American assault troops lie huddled on the shingle of Omaha Assault Area, surrounded by their equipment, as exhausted, shocked survivors look on. According to Watkinson, *Belfast* went down to Omaha Assault Area at the end of June.

There was one little incident ... the weather turned out a bit nice and we were standing on the decks and we still had half the company at action stations ... and there was a big launch full of war correspondents ... They were alongside and one of the 6-inch guns was facing shoreward and the marines had a dart board and they were playing darts. All of a sudden the gun went off ... and all these correspondents in the launch all rushed up on deck thinking the ship had blown up. And ... later on we got the *Daily Mirror* with 'HMS *Belfast* fires its guns while the Royal Marines are playing darts' sent in by one of the correspondents!

Later, Peter Brooke Smith related with relish how he finally fired in anger for the first time the Oerlikon with which he had been playing in his free time, missing a Messerschmitt 110 which was really a long way out of range. The following day, after a night broken by a violent skirmish between light coastal forces and German E-boats, at the end of which the destroyer HMS *Stevenstone* reported sinking one enemy craft, the terrifying rocket-landing craft were deployed again, five in total letting fly. They were still impressive more than two weeks after the *Belfast* men had first seen them. Bob Shrimpton commented: 'These things going off like darts. Incredible. The firepower ... was out of this world!'

With *Belfast* virtually immobile now, moored opposite Sword beach, the air threat much reduced, and the fighting ashore largely out of range of her secondary guns, many of her ship's company were woefully underemployed, including Charles Simpson's engine room team:

We became from the military point of view less and less concerned because the fighting going further and further from the coast required guns with a range of 12 miles less and less ... our duties then became local. The majority of the ship's company were landed in parties to perform duties ashore. Most of the stokers went on shore with sailors, seamen and gunnery ratings as a combined party to do duties of rescue and restoration on land.

Simpson went on to relate how one of his stokers brought him back a tropical plant, salvaged from a ruined house as a gift. For David Jones, and some of the other men who were unwillingly dragged from their sunbathing on 23 June to fetch and carry ashore, the experience was less than inspiring: 'I went out with a beach clearance party', he related tersely, 'We went ashore on an American duck ... [We were] just trying to move vehicles out the way and this kind of thing and helping generally.

There was a Beachmaster there ... he was a Lieutenant-Commander I think. "Do this, do that, push that, shove that!" We didn't know what we was achieving really, we just did what we were told!'

Jones was probably not best qualified to comment on the Beachmasters' role, which was in reality absolutely essential. To make the enormous task marginally more manageable, each of the five principal invasion beaches was divided into sectors and then subdivided again into smaller beach areas, which became the responsibility of a Beachmaster. Lieutenant Edward Guerritz was the Principal Beachmaster on Red Beach, Queen Sector, Sword Beach, and he summed up his extensive responsibilities admirably:

Above: 'I went out with a beach clearance party ... there was a Beachmaster there ... "Do this, do that, push that shove that!" We didn't know what we was achieving really, we just did what we were told!' – David Jones. The Beachmaster's Headquarters near Courseulles. According to the original caption the Naval Commandos in the party include B C Lambert, RNVR, of Bromley, Kent; Sub-Lieutenant Parsey, of Bradford, Yorkshire; and Leading Seaman Springall, of Poplar, London.

The task of the Beach Group which was the military element centred on an infantry battalion and it had added to it engineer, medical transport RAF and naval components to enable it to carry out all the necessary duties of receiving men and vehicles from the landing craft and ships, clearing them through the beach exits into transit areas, and either then to storage depots or through to the operational front. So the naval beach party element of this...was to provide navigational marks to assist in the clearance of obstacles below the high water mark, to mark any obstructions...and generally to provide the incoming landing craft with as much guidance as possible and to expedite the unloading of...personnel, vehicles or stores and clear them off the beach as quickly as possible...it's never straightforward! Things don't go particularly well in exercise and it doesn't help when you're being shot at as well. The point is that we had considerable difficulty in clearing the vehicles off the beach in our area, partly because of mining by the Germans and partly that we were victims of our own success in getting a large amount of stuff ashore and the exits were ill-suited to the volume of traffic we could provide...but mines were one of the chief hazards and of course vehicles do break down or 'drown' as the expression is. You can also create quicksand due to gunfire the sand [becomes] quicksand. We had to close our beach for a period because of the difficulty of dispersing the vehicles.

Below: 'They sent us ashore to do a bit of clearing up on the beaches – Gordon Painter.
A wrecked British M5 Stuart light tank sits forlornly in the Normandy shallows, with another half-drowned tank and two beached LSTs in the background.

For David Jones, even being shelled on the beach was just another normal day's work: 'We were getting shelled all the time, just this one gun. It would only be a couple of shells a day, they'd come whistling over and bang! Bit disconcerting. When we were on the beach … the shells were exploding fairly near to us and they were shooting at the beach at that time. Didn't get hurt though.'

Gordon Painter was another man who was sent ashore, remembering the experience matter-of-factly:

They sent us ashore to do a bit of clearing up on the beaches. There wasn't a lot, I mean the main clearing up had been done. Casualty wise I think the medical people had done that before we got there … There was all sorts of things, parts of ships that had been broken up, GI's equipment that they'd lost. I assume a lot of the soldiers had been killed and lost their gear.

Painter was one of those who found time to poke around in the shell-torn houses which lined the beach. Most of the really good souvenirs had long since been stripped out by the troops, but he did pick up, bizarrely, 'a couple of pictures of Shirley Temple', and some German letters which were later translated by the ship's 'Schoolie', Instructor-Lieutenant D M McPhee, MA. Peter Brooke Smith transcribed a couple of the letters for his diary, achingly sad messages from home recording a miserable, dangerous, wearying wartime existence of rationing and relentless bombing, which was little different to the experience of families in Britain or any other country. 'My dear Willi', wrote Marrla from Cologne on 5 May, 'Here it is worse than ever, we don't have any peace now, day or night. No-one thinks of going to bed before 2 o'clock in the morning. Since the last big raid I am so worried that I don't go to bed at all ... I think I have been bewildered by the bombs'. Reading them now, years later, it is still almost impossible not to wonder whether Marrla and Willi survived the war, or not to imagine that some *Belfast* men must have wondered the same.

Denis Watkinson remembered more of the experience of working ashore. According to him, the first time the landing party set out, the officer in charge aborted the entire expedition, much to everyone's relief:

Below: As the beaches became safer, it was possible to set up more sophisticated medical facilities, like No. 88 General Hospital at Douvres-la-Délivrande, where this cheerful group of nurses from Queen Alexandra's Imperial Military Nursing Service has just arrived. The first nurses went to Normandy just days after D-Day. Today Douvres-la-Délivrande is the site of a Commonwealth War Graves Commission cemetery; doubtless these determined young women tended some of the occupants in their last hours.

One day we were picked ... there must have been about 50 of us altogether. And he says 'You're going ashore at Sword beach to try and help them, because the beach is getting littered with getting shelled regular, so they can get stuff in'. We got in these launches ... when we came to where the ships were ... you could see the shelling ... So the officer in charge says 'look we're not going to make it', so we went back to the ship and I thought 'thank God for that!'

Unfortunately for Watkinson, the relentless pressure of naval orders was not to be defied. The next morning, the landing party was ordered to fall in again: 'Oh God here we go again', Watkinson remembered thinking as they boarded a motor launch and headed for the shore.

As they passed between the Gooseberry breakwater into the Mulberry harbour, the anchorage came under German fire. For Watkinson, it was the first time at Normandy that he felt genuinely frightened – out of his element, exposed and under fire:

> I can honestly say you're a bit apprehensive, no doubt, but I never had fear until I got on that [boat]. I had no gun to fire back, I was on a small boat, being shelled and couldn't do nothing about it … it's the only time I can honestly say I was afraid because they could see me and they could shoot me and I couldn't fire back … There was more boats from other ships, all trying to help out … there was one got hit just further up from us. I lay down on the bottom and I prayed, I did, I prayed. You know when they say when you're drowning you think about your family, your past and everything comes up and it did with me.

Inside the harbour, the seamen were transferred to a DUKW, driven, doubtless to their considerable distress, by a disturbingly cheerful soldier:

> As we got round the bend, the army came with the … ducks. He says, 'right, jump in here and we'll get you ashore!' There was a bit of a smokescreen but there wasn't much and we got in these boats and the lad driving he says, 'lie down in the bottom as much as you can, we'll get ashore don't worry'. So he did, he got us ashore … so we get on the beach and I kissed the sand! I said 'thank God for that'.

More than two weeks after D-Day, Sword beach was still very much on the front line, dangerous and confusing. As the bewildered sailors listened to the Beachmaster deliver terrifying warnings about mines and other hazards, they watched miserably as a stark-naked sailor struggled ashore, a survivor from the launch which had been hit as they arrived. It was not the best start to their excursion. Watkinson describes how, fortunately, their own officer had more sympathy for their situation and his own:

Below: 'The army came with the … ducks. He says "right jump in here and we'll get you ashore! The lad driving he says "lie down in the bottom as much as you can, we'll get ashore don't worry". So we get on the beach and I kissed the sand!' – Denis Watkinson.
In the shelter of the Mulberry harbour at Arromanches, cargo is transferred in nets from a coaster into a 'Duck' (DUKW).

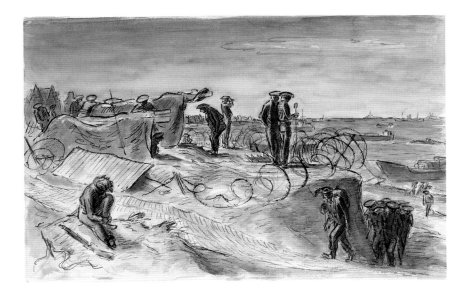

So the officer says ... 'Try and get as near the water's edge as you can and anything that shifts, try and shift it and we'll take it inland' ... We all lined up and as soon as we went in, out come the shells ... they were getting nearer and nearer, so he says, 'Right, make your way back to the top of the beach, we can't work here, it's hopeless! It's no good getting yourself killed, just for trying to pull these bits and pieces clear.'

The *Belfast* working party trudged further up the beach, where they started to clear random debris from the beach, 'bits falling off boats and floating in off the tide you know, quite a few things', and to load it into a borrowed army lorry. Once the vehicle was full, they drove along a narrow Norman lane to a field full of wrecked German war material. Watkinson recalled:

I always remember turning and there was a big field, it was where they were dumping all the German stuff. I always remember seeing a [tiny] German tank ... There was a few of them, and what they were, were 'beetle' tanks and they used to radio control them and blow them when they got anywhere near you. They were marvellous things ... a proper tank, tracks on and everything.

As the sweating sailors heaved scrap from the truck and carried it, panting, into the field, they were given a chilling warning by a passing

soldier: 'Don't go too far up there', he called casually, 'there's snipers up there!' 'Oh God', Watkinson thought, 'that's all we need'. Lunch was some tins brought out from the ship, eaten on tin plates which had to be scrubbed clean in the sand. The tired sailors found a wooden beach hut, piled inside and flopped down on the floor. As they munched away thoughtfully, a very young soldier sidled up to chat: 'I always remember an army lad coming up to us and he said "I'm lost", and I think he was one that had got a bit frightened and he said have you got any cigarettes ... I think he'd done a bunk.' After a meagre lunch, there was time to explore the shell-torn houses along the waterfront, and for some souvenir hunting. The line between souvenir hunting and looting is of course a fine one – 'looting' is generally recorded as being carried out by the other side. In this case it was universally, and almost certainly unfairly, blamed on the Canadians aboard:

> There was a row of houses and we went in one of these. They were lovely houses, they hadn't been up long ... and I got a magazine dated the day before, I took that with us. There was one lad ... he went up into the loft there and he found a double-barrelled shotgun in a case. He was a Canadian, and he took that.

According to Watkinson, another supposed 'Canadian' had a strange predilection for liberating the wooden cats and other animals which

Above left: 'On the shore was a row of houses with ... evidence of defence. There were millions of crossed bits of steel bars lying on the sand. In the sea there were innumerable landing craft.' – Charles Simpson.
Ink drawing by Edward James, entitled 'LCTs Ram the Beach to Bring in Supplies: the Royal Dragoon Guards Attacking the Defences'. The nearest LCT has been damaged.

Above right: As the fighting moved inland from the beachheads, the Allies were able to establish airfields in Normandy, bringing the deadly fighter bombers much nearer to the front line. Chalk drawing by Stephen Bone of an LST loaded with RAF motor transport, mostly fuel tankers, nearing France. Airmen are lining the rails.

decorated the gables of the Norman beach houses. But the carnival atmosphere was largely illusory. On Sword beach the front line was just a few miles away, and the beach and anchorage were under constant shell fire:

> Further over there was a landing stage sticking out ... and a boat was unloading. It was only a small boat, and over the top of us, you could hear them fire and you could hear it going over the top of us, and [it] hit that, it didn't half hit it! You couldn't do anything unless you did it quick and got off, if you did anything that took more than a few minutes.

At the end of the day, the beach party piled gratefully back into their DUKW and left the bleak, war-torn Norman shore, gratefully settling back inside *Belfast*'s reassuringly thick steel hull. Denis Watkinson, much to his relief, did not have to return.

The safety of the ship was to an extent illusory. The next day, 24 June, the *Belfast* men were shocked from their confident complacency by a graphic illustration that the gunline was still the front line, and a very dangerous place indeed. At 07:30, a brief log entry notes: '*Swift* mined

Above: On 6 June 1944, Anthony Gross accompanied troops of the Royal Army Service Corps to Normandy. He landed at Gold Beach near Bayeux with the 50th (Northumberland) Division. While awaiting his turn to land, he made a series of pencil sketches of troops disembarking on the beaches. Two hours later, he jumped into the sea with his watercolours and paper held over his head.

A 715054
Swift
S.Ph. to Press 326
R/S. Ph. 7.1.44

and sinking' (Log 1). The men who witnessed the tragedy remembered it in far more graphic detail, even years later, although typically when remembering an event which happened with such terrible suddenness, they remember different aspects of it or even remember it in different ways. For Larry Fursland, it was short, and vivid:

> I was at my vantage point having a fag before I went down for the forenoon when a destroyer came past about 50 yards away, men on the upper deck giving the V-sign ... there was a terrific explosion, before I had another drag of my fag all that was left was the crosstrees of the mast. It was the destroyer called *Swift*.

Lance Tyler remembered the same things with slightly more measured detail. *Swift*, he recalled, 'had gone out and done circuits and bumps to

Above: 'There was a terrific explosion, before I had another drag of my fag all that was left was the cross trees of the mast.' – Larry Fursland.
The destroyer HMS *Swift*, photographed in the Solent in January 1944. An officer and 17 men lost their lives when she detonated a mine and sank on 24 June 1944.

have a look for U-boats or anything like that that might be causing trouble between Portsmouth and Normandy and she came back [and] she dropped her anchor'. According to Tyler, *Belfast* came very close to sharing the same fate, claiming that if the two ships had swung in opposite directions on their cables then *Belfast* would have struck the mine. Tyler also recalled a dramatic lower-deck 'buzz' about an eccentric *Swift* seaman: 'Rumour had it that there was a three badge Able Seaman on board HMS *Swift* who suddenly realised that he'd left his wallet [behind] so he … swam back, clambered on board, got his wallet and then came back and away.'

Andy Palmer, an experienced watch-keeping officer, also believed *Belfast* had a narrow escape, remembering with the detail typical of a trained observer. According to Palmer, *Belfast* had recently shifted her berth to take up a new bombardment position and was about to open fire when *Swift* passed across her stern. Palmer had a theory about why *Belfast* escaped:

As she passed *Belfast*'s stern she exploded a mine which broke her in two. And there was this splendid destroyer just gone like that … she folded. Amazing. What was really amazing was the fact that our stern must have passed over that mine not long before, but I suppose we were saved by the … counter-mechanism. The Germans would protect their mines so they wouldn't fire the first time by the approach of a minesweeper, they would fire on the target vessel following the minesweeper and I suppose that was what saved the *Belfast* on that occasion.

Bob Shrimpton went out with one of *Belfast*'s boat crews to try and rescue the survivors:

The order went out 'sea boats away', and I went out with Number 1 boat. The ship was already sinking bow first and I remember seeing the ship's crew just sort of stepping off. One chap had a Burberry over one arm and a suitcase in his other arm and he just sort of stepped into the water … And another lad had lost quite a lot of the upper part of his body [which] had been caught by the blast. And we took them back to the ship and up through scramble nets to get them aboard. That was not a very pleasant thing, I forget how many were lost but that wasn't a very pleasant morning.

For Charles Simpson, also on deck at the time, the loss of *Swift* was a moment for reflection and empathy: 'My own feelings as I watched it sink beneath the waves was sorrow at all their personal possessions being drowned', he recalled, 'This was it, this was war, this was what we'd come for. When you see a ship gradually sink beneath the waves you think of a sailor's home being destroyed.'

Peter Brooke Smith recorded the event in his diary, dated 24 June: 'At 07:20 the destroyer *Swift* went up on a mine 2 cables on our port bow. Broke her back but the two ends remained afloat for some time and the mast still shows even at high water. Motor boat lowered and sent for casualties with creditable despatch.' The log records that *Belfast*'s boats returned towing three rafts full of survivors and that other men were picked up from the water; 44 men died. Lieutenant-Commander J R Gower was *Swift*'s commanding officer, and described the exact circumstances of the loss of his ship in his memoirs years later (see Primary Sources, IWM Department of Documents):

> With a number of other destroyers we went out on E-boat patrol at dusk and soon after midnight the alarm was raised. I spotted three or four but they were difficult to identify and each side fired at each other without much success. On returning to harbour to go alongside HMS *Scourge* next morning at 07:00 and going very slowly because of the laying of the new German ... mine, we suddenly felt an enormous thump and sure enough we'd been unlucky enough to activate one. The explosion was underneath the bridge and forward boiler room, which broke the back of the ship. A subsequent count ... resulted in 1 officer and 17 men losing their lives. There were also quite a number of broken limbs because the upward impact below threw several people several feet into the air ... my Yeoman of Signals was blown over the side. The impact was so great because of the shallow water and eventually the ship was left with her bow and stern clearly visible but the midships section submerged.

Lieutenant-Commander Gower returned to the UK on 14 days survivors' leave, where he learned that he had been awarded the Distinguished Service Cross for his command of *Swift* during Operation 'Overlord'. His destroyer was not the only casualty on 24 June. Five minutes later, a big transport struck a mine a mile away from *Belfast*. Peter Brooke Smith described it in vivid detail:

> A merchant ship on our starboard quarter went up and her stern broke off abaft her funnel. These Liberty Ships split easily. One of her cargo of lorries caught fire and soon a big oil fire was blazing in her bunkers. Fire floats eventually put it out, but the huge column of black smoke that billowed up

for hours must have been of great satisfaction to the Germans for miles around.

This was perhaps the incident remembered slightly differently by Bernard Thomson. There is no doubt that serious explosions and fire could seem much worse than they actually were, although it seems odd that neither Brooke Smith nor the ship's log record a ship actually sinking:

> One day this big gun [sic] hit the deck of a big merchant ship ... and it hit a wagon which was on the top, full of ammunition, which blew the bow away and it started to sink. That must have been a 10,000 tonner ship, it was very big and it was loaded with troops, their weapons, wagon, tanks everything and that went straight down more or less, went down within five minutes. The fleet sent all the boats it could, there was a special announcement from the captain all boats to be manned and off they went to try and save who they could.

According to Brooke Smith, 200 soldiers had been trapped below decks at breakfast and died, although this has been impossible to substantiate. As the day wore on, German coastal guns scored hits on a transport ship and the landing craft (gun) *LCG 11*, struck by German counter-battery fire as she was bombarding close inshore. The same gun battery then shifted fire to *Belfast* and the other cruisers, prompting Parham to shift his berth and move out of range. Later that night, a 'tip and run' raider dropped a bomb just under a mile off *Belfast*'s starboard bow and shortly afterwards a pair of Junkers 188 bombers passed straight over, dropping more bombs on the starboard side. The battle was certainly not over.

The troublesome German battery which hit the transport and *LCG 11* was creeping steadily closer to *Belfast*. On 25 June, it scored a hit on the transport *Cap Touraine*, killing two Royal Marines. *Belfast* did not return fire; log entries for the day record absolutely no 'shoots' at all, just a couple of air raid warnings and visits by two landing craft hoping to top up their fresh water supplies. At 16:15 the following day, Parham finally lost patience with the vicious German guns when they opened fire on

Above: 'An army corporal had been badly blown up and they were trying to save this man's life.' – Lance Tyler.
Wounded soldiers are gently carried on stretchers from an ambulance, through the bow doors into the welcome embrace of an LCT, in this drawing by Stephen Bone.

the Gooseberries breakwater and *Belfast* targeted the battery with a full broadside. Otherwise the day was once again uneventful. Peter Brooke Smith could find nothing to write about at all, other than, cryptically, receiving a 'letter from Stockholm'. 27 June passed entirely uneventfully, as did the 28 June, although the night was a busy one. The log records a relentless stream of air raid alerts and aircraft sightings, along with full umbrella barrages just after midnight and again at 00:35. The anti-aircraft cruiser HMS *Argonaut* scored a hit during the latter, prompting an outburst of jealousy by Brooke Smith. '*Argonaut* shot plane down in ball of flame', he wrote, 'Damn her! It would have walked into our barrage otherwise.'

This response might seem inappropriate today, but it is important to remember that by 1944, Britain was exhausted by nearly five years of war against an unrelenting and ruthless foe. Her cities had been bombed, her armies defeated and her merchant shipping stalked and sent to the bottom in an attempt to starve her people into surrender. The only successes had been scored in the Mediterranean, far from home. For many *Belfast*

Above: The Landing in Normandy: Arromanches, D-Day plus 20, 26th June 1944, by Barnett Freedman. This extraordinarily detailed panoramic oil painting vividly conveys the hive of activity which Arromanches had become by the end of June, with Mulberry B completed and operational. Creating a huge, complex port, in what was to all intents and purposes the 'middle of nowhere' in industrial terms, was an engineering achievement which cannot be overstated.

men, this was the first time they had seen the enemy on the back foot. Leslie Coleman put it succinctly, for him the war was very personal: 'My brother had come back from Dunkirk, whether that made any difference I don't know ... [but] I felt really good. "Now we're getting our own back", that's the way I felt about it.'

In any case, the battle was still by no means one-sided. On 29 June, Peter Brooke Smith noted in his diary that *Belfast*'s officers had entertained the officers of a visiting LCT in the wardroom. The peaceful murmur of conversation and the clink of glasses had been interrupted at 20:30 when the troublesome German coastal battery opened fire, this time almost certainly at *Belfast*. When the cruiser was shaken violently by a very near miss, the landing craft officers hurriedly downed their drinks and took their ship away. The rugged little steel 'shoe box' was some 20 yards off *Belfast*'s port quarter when disaster struck. Peter Brooke Smith was watching from the gun deck:

'Heard the whistle of the next one coming ... it hit the LCT, which had just shoved off, just below the bridge ... Motor Boat came up for doctor, urgently. Our doctors ready to go but we had to send the boat to *Argonaut* as we were under weigh.'

Brooke Smith learned later that the LCT's commanding officer, only recently sipping gin in *Belfast*'s wardroom, had lost a leg and later died. *Belfast*'s turn came on the next day, 30 June, incidentally the day the Allies felt secure enough in their Normandy beachhead to declare Operation 'Neptune' to be over. The problems began when the troublesome battery, which was located near Le Havre, opened fire again. The log entry was typically brief, '11:30. Shells from shore falling close', but it masks a moment of genuine drama which many of the ship's company recalled clearly (Log 1). The relentless shellfire had already prompted some caution on Parham's part. 'If you're fired on, which you were fired on regular,' Denis Watkinson remembered, 'the anchor party used to go and pull the ship up by the anchor so that you took them off target. You didn't move very far, just enough.'

'Buzzes' had already begun to circulate, speculating on the nature of the mysterious gun. Most of the sailors believed it was some sort of railway gun, hidden in a tunnel when it was not firing, and in fact a large German railway gun was later captured near Le Havre. It was perhaps the regular, seemingly unpreventable nature of the shellfire which was the most exhausting, rather than the actual hits caused, which were rare. Boy Seaman David Jones' story is typical. 'We were under shell fire for about 30 odd days', he remembered, 'there was one single gun. I heard ... afterwards that it was mounted on a railway truck and it used to back into a tunnel ... come out, fire a couple of shots and back in the tunnel again, and this had gone on for about 30 odd days'. Jones concluded with the typical and impressive understatement that 'It was a bit wearing you know, shells exploding here and there'.

Larry Fursland related what happened at 11:30 on 30 June in typical style:

> This one [shell] came right near the ship ... the shell exploded before it struck the ship. The shrapnel went through ... and the butchers' shop was around there with these two marines ... and the shrapnel penetrated there and one lost a leg and the other died since ... when you look at the foremost funnel ... there's a couple of patches on that funnel and that's where the shrapnel went through.

Peter Brooke Smith was another man who was matter-of-fact about the near miss. 'Right ... short... over. The short spattered shrapnel over ship. Wounded the butcher, an E.R.A [Engine Room Artificer], and a lookout.' He even went on to note that he found the regular shelling 'quite exciting'. Denis Watkinson was rather nearer to the explosion, on stand-by watch and asleep between 4-inch firings inside P1 Gun Crew Shelter:

> All of a sudden there was an almighty bang and ringing right throughout, and I thought 'Oh God we've been hit again!' Opened the door, air it was like snow, paint going down, and there was big hole in the funnel. It must have exploded ... and below that was the beef screen and the marine was in there and he got badly injured in there, they took him, I don't know what actually happened to him ... Went through there, went through the funnel and we never got one bit. There was a lad further down he was on lookout down the aft end of the ship and he got some shrapnel in him.

But for one man, the shell was a very personal near-death experience. By now,

Below: 'There was one single gun. I heard ... afterwards that it was mounted on a railway truck and it used to back into a tunnel.'
– David Jones.
Watercolour by C A Russell of a camouflaged German railway gun, captured near Le Havre. Perhaps this was the gun which caused HMS *Belfast* so much trouble!

Bernard Thomson had resumed his duties as an Officer's Cook. Only a small quantity of stores were kept in his tiny galley, and his job involved repeated trips to a store to replenish: 'Potatoes used to come from just behind the bridge. There used to be … a meat and vegetable locker where they used to deep freeze a lot of stuff and two Royal Marines used to look after it, they used to call them Marine butchers.' Thomson was on his way to the Meat Locker on the morning of 30 June, when he was accosted by an irate Petty Officer:

> I was going to the potato locker to get this meat and this Petty Officer said to me 'Chef where's your lifebelt … you know you're at Action Stations'. The Captain had decided to halve the ship, port and starboard, one lot on action stations and one lot doing their normal duties … anyway I was on the part that wasn't at action stations, on my normal duties because the officers were getting a bit peckish, they were getting sick of iron rations … Anyway he said 'where's your lifebelt chef?'

Thomson was presumably bewildered. Parham's compromise solution, whilst necessary to maintain morale and keep up regular routines over such a long period in action, could be confusing for men who had been trained to live their lives to a strict routine. 'I said it's in the mess', he remembered, 'He said "you'll have to get it, you know, be a good lad and go and get it and put it on."' Thomson returned to his mess deck and retrieved his lifejacket. Almost immediately – within 15 seconds according to Thomson – there was huge explosion alongside the ship as the shell landed alongside the ship's port side, four feet from where Thomson stood. He emerged to chaos:

> When the bang went off the bugle went 'action stations' again and … 'medical staff report on the port side', and all sorts of orders because of the damage from the shell. I came out the mess, started walking back towards the galley past the potato locker and two sailors were dragging one of the marines, his leg was nearly blown off, and another sailor had a towel or something on his head.

Thomson was immediately and chillingly aware that he had had a very narrow escape:

Now I would have been larking on with the Royal Marines getting my meat ... [The] shell landed right where I [would have been] standing ... the potato locker. It splattered all the railings and the 4-inch gun emplacement up above and the two Royal Marines inside. One nearly lost his leg and the other one was badly injured and several sailors who'd been manning guns ... in that section of the ship had been hit with shrapnel.

Years later, he was still absolutely convinced that he had escaped death or serious injury by the narrowest of margins: 'When I came out ... I never did go and get the meat! I went back to the galley and I was petrified because I could have been killed. And I've that Petty Officer to thank for making me go and get my lifebelt. This all happened within a minute of leaving the spot where I was stood.'

The night of 30 June/1 July was eventful, broken by air raids, umbrella barrages, gunfire ashore and searchlights, along with friendly Stirling aircraft flying over to drop supplies to the troops, an interesting illustration of the constant risk of 'friendly fire' incidents. At 02:10, Peter Brooke Smith finally thought he had succeeded in obtaining the anti-aircraft 'kill' for which he had been waiting so long:

A plane was shot down and we picked up another in searchlights. Although the guns were slow in opening fire, had a good long run and radar plot. Got bursts near. The plane (Ju 188 or He 111) crashed in flames and burned on water for some time. We can justly claim a share though there was lots of stuff going up. We were the last to be seen firing at it before it crashed.

Certainly, Brooke Smith felt confident enough to put in an official claim for the kill the next day. By July, it is notable from the log entries that *Belfast* was firing her main armament on fewer and fewer occasions, and air attacks during the day had become incredibly rare. 2 July was almost entirely uneventful, Peter Brooke Smith noting briefly that he was 'rather out of step now', before going on to report gratefully that *Belfast* was due to return to the UK for a long refit in a few days' time. The next day Brooke Smith simply wrote 'life the same', although at 05:45 on 3 July a log entry noted a sighting of what was almost certainly a V1 'flying bomb': 'pilotless aircraft passed astern' (Log 2).

Tuesday 4 July was livelier. With the Stars and Stripes flying in honour of US Independence Day and the crew sunbathing and playing deck games, a lone Messerschmitt 110 appeared, ablaze and being pursued by Spitfires. Brooke Smith described vividly how 'its wings eventually broke off and fluttered down', before the aircraft crashed in flames near Ouistreham. Later that night there was a particularly close brush with the ever-present German E-boats, which Captain Parham remembered only too well: 'I remember one evening we and one other ship were all alone down the eastern end and quite unprotected ... and about 3 or 4 miles further west was where the merchant ships all congregated and one or two other bombardment ships with them and they were always very nicely covered by a splendid smokescreen all night'. Wisely he suggested to Dalrymple-Hamilton that perhaps *Belfast* might take advantage of this:

> I suggested to my admiral that here we were now and the moon was once again full ... and we were sticking out like haystacks down the eastern end. Wouldn't it be quite a good idea, even though we had to do it very slowly, to get up under the cover of this smokescreen? And my admiral looked at me I think rather as if he thought I'd got cold feet (which of course I had!) but eventually agreed and so we moved up very very slowly and joined the throng under this nice protective smokescreen ... we used to listen in to the German wireless telegraphing between the motor torpedo boats and so on which had come out for us. And we actually heard one evening one chap telling another in German exactly where the *Belfast* was by name. And it was where we were but fortunately we were not there then.

Peter Brooke Smith noted the same incident in his diary: 'Moved with great caution, to prevent sending up pressure mines, to other anchorage at dusk. Just as well, for it was this night two E-boats were overheard talking on the RT: where is the *verdammte Belfast*?' The night was a disturbed one, with four Red air raid alerts between midnight and 01:30. Brooke Smith spent it uncomfortably perched on the rangefinder in the director, trying unsuccessfully to sleep. At this point in the campaign the Kriegsmarine introduced another threat into the mix, resorting to what they called their *kleinkampfverbände* (small battle units), initially human torpedoes and Linsen explosive motor boats. These were really weapons of desperation rather than ingenuity, deployed with half-trained teenage operators by a service which had lost nearly all of its significant naval units and essentially had no effective way of countering the overwhelming sea power the Allies deployed off Normandy. However, although they claimed few actual victims they formed a fairly constant source of anxiety for the men aboard the bigger and less manoeuvrable ships. Peter Brooke

Smith recorded his first human torpedo scare on 6 July, and the log for the night of 5/6 July is peppered with references to human torpedo sightings; this was in fact the first serious assault on the fleet by a force of 40 human torpedoes despatched from a firing point in Favrol Woods. They sank two minesweepers, HMS *Magic* and HMS *Cato*, but all but nine of the human torpedoes were lost.

Bob Shrimpton remembered a novel method of protecting *Belfast* against such weapons:

> Later on ... they had a threat from these human torpedoes, the German Navy coming out of Brest and ... there was a very crude answer to that and that was for the sea boat to go out with a Gunnery Officer or a Petty Officer on board with a box of hand grenades. They would just sail slowly round the ship and if they saw anything suspicious just throw a hand grenade in the water and we all thought 'what a wonderful waste of ammunition'.

Below: 'Later on ... they had a threat from these human torpedoes, the German Navy coming out of Brest.' – Bob Shrimpton.
A German lorry carrying a standard G7e naval torpedo, captured by Polish soldiers near Falaise. The improvised human torpedoes used one of these weapons as a crude submersible, complete with a basic cockpit fitted with rudimentary controls and a plexiglass dome to allow the operator to see. A live torpedo was slung underneath. They were far more dangerous to their operators than the Allies.

Peter Brooke Smith also described dropping 5-pound explosive charges from boats as 'anti-human torpedo and infernal machine measure'. Bernard Thomson remembered 'Americans' in motor boats doing much the same thing, using 'some kind of small depth charges like a hand grenade'. He also remembered evidence of their effectiveness:

A few days later we saw some bodies floating in the sea. We were told they were ... German midget submariners [who] had been trying to put limpet charges on the ship ... I don't know if they had been lucky or not but ... these poor German sailors they didn't last, they was unlucky ... [These sights] were very new to me, luckily we was young and we were fighting ... we just thought we were there fighting for our country and the sight, it didn't make us sick or anything but it was a bit [of a] peculiar feeling went through your body thinking it could have been you. But other than that we just got on with our work and carried on.

Dropping grenades in the water was not the only precaution that Captain Parham could take. He also sent down the ship's divers to check her bottom, and also instructed a team of Royal Marines to drag her. Denis Watkinson watched them at work:

What they were doing, there were one man subs or whatever they were, they were sticking, we called them sticky bombs, on the ships' bottoms. So ... one day ... we got a wire cable, dropped it down the forecastle, got all hands that they could get and pulled that wire the full length of the ship to scrape anything that was on the bottom of the ship ... because they had sunk a couple of ships doing that, putting these sticky bombs on it.

Soon afterwards *Belfast*'s men witnessed the beginning of the end of the battle for Caen, on 7 July, when, at the start of Montgomery's offensive codenamed Operation 'Charnwood', hundreds of heavy bombers levelled the

Below: Belfast's last battle. Sherman tanks of 33rd Armoured Brigade, supporting 3rd Infantry Division, moving forward near Lebisey Wood for Operation 'Charnwood', the assault on Caen, 8 July 1944. The cruiser weighed anchor and left for home for the last time as Montgomery's armour was rolling down this dusty Norman road.

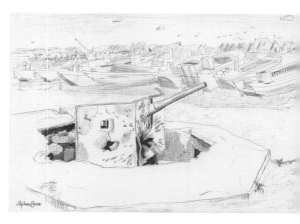

city, allowing British and Canadian soldiers to successfully storm it from three sides and establish a bridgehead south of the River Odon. Brooke Smith wrote:

> During the first [watch] a most impressive spectacle as Lancasters (there seemed over a thousand – the BBC later said 450) went over in one long stream, fairly low, lasting an hour, to bomb Caen and the front to west of Caen. Gave it hell. Lot of small flak but only three seemed to be hit and only one brought down. The whole thing a most shattering spectacle. Watched markers go down and then the whole area was shrouded in dust and smoke.

The spectacle impressed all who saw it. Bob Shrimpton described the sky as 'black ... that morning, the air, you couldn't see it, it was just one mass of aircraft ...' Denis Watkinson recalled Captain Parham telling his crew what was going on and encouraging them to come on deck and watch:

> 'If you take a look in a certain direction', Parham announced over the ship's tannoy system, 'you'll see about 500 bombers'...They were house top height, they were low, very low ... 'Take notice they're all British', says our skipper, and obviously we were in line with Caen ... They got to Caen and like a wall of fire came up ... and the anti-aircraft fire was going like a big flame and the lads were just going in and the ship was vibrating, our ship was vibrating with the weight of what them bombers [dropped] ... You thought God help them poor people.

One of Watkinson's friends apparently went into Caen not long after, reporting back, shocked, that he had 'never seen anything like it'.

Larry Fursland described the scene with typical verve, preferring, like many of the sailors, to believe that there actually were a thousand heavy bombers. 'All I saw was waves', he remembered,

> They started off with a thousand bomber raid ... after a while the Captain [said] 'Clear lower deck everyone ... and come and see some British planes for a bloody change!'... Cor what a bloody din ... you saw first of all our English fighter pilots, what guts they had! They were there, some was ablazing, still going on ... in particular two planes I saw were wholly ablaze and still they carried on ... As they were coming I saw the bomb doors open.

Ron Jesse was equally impressed. There could have been no better demonstration of the overwhelming Allied air superiority at this stage in the war. Few of the watching sailors could have been left in any doubt that victory must surely be inevitable:

> I remember the thousand bomber raid that went over, plane after plane after plane in formation one after the other and they went over ... and in the distance you could see the tinsel falling which was a radar blind. Each aeroplane dropped its little bits of tinfoil, aluminium foil to battle the enemy's radar and then 'boom boom boom!' They were bombing somewhere inland, with a thousand bombers, it was tremendous.

According to the ship's log, this raid began at 21:37: 'large flight of Lancasters with fighter escort passed overhead and commenced bombing the coast. Estimated 1,000 bombers bombing Caen'. (Log 2)

Operation 'Charnwood' was one of the last actions in which *Belfast* directly participated. On the following day, Saturday 8 July 1944, the cruiser received orders to return to the UK. But the anchorage still remained lethal to the unwary or unlucky, and even on their last day on the gunline, the *Belfast* men witnessed some dreadful sights. During the night of 7/8 July, the Kriegsmarine launched their second (and final) assault on the anchorage, using 21 of the human torpedoes. This time they scored a notable success; at 04:34 a determined human torpedo 'pilot' pressed home an attack on the old Polish cruiser *Dragon*, originally built for the Royal Navy back in 1917, when she had been the fastest ship in the fleet. Although not sunk *Dragon* was very badly damaged, with a 5m by 15m hole in her side and her magazines and engine room flooded. Her guns were removed, she was decommissioned and then eventually scuttled as part of

Far left: 'Lancasters ... went over in one long stream, fairly low, lasting an hour, to bomb Caen and the front to west of Caen. Gave it hell.' – Peter Brooke Smith.
The shattered ruins of Caen, by war artist Stephen Bone, drawn in August 1944. Operation 'Charnwood' ended when British and Canadian troops entered the city on 9 July 1944. The victory cost nearly 4,000 Allied dead. Caen was supposed to have been taken on D-Day, but it took over a month of bitter fighting to reach the city.

Left: Aftermath: A shell-torn, rusting German 50mm kwk 39 anti-tank gun in an emplacement at Courseulles, drawn in chalk by Stephen Bone. Symbolically, the captured, harmless weapon is pointing impotently to the sky in front of a triumphant row of landing craft, drawn up on the beach. Remarkably this gun can still be seen in Normandy, exhibiting the same damage it does in Bone's drawing.

the Gooseberry breakwater off Courseulles. 26 men died. The attack was attributed to a human torpedo pilot named Walter Gerhold, who was decorated with the Knight's Cross, one of Germany's highest awards for gallantry. (Gerhold died in 2013 aged 91. There is apparently some doubt over his involvement; other sources cite a junior officer named Midshipman Potthast, who also survived and was taken prisoner by the British.)

Dragon's record-breaking days were long behind her. She was really too old for front line service by 1944, and Peter Brooke Smith, for one, was disgusted. He recorded his outrage for posterity: 'Wretched *Dragon* hit by mine or torpedo and towed in to be made part of Mulberry. For what use that old thing is she might just as well have not been here. Is an insult to the Poles who have been given her to man, and is just throwing away lives.'

Later that night, Brooke Smith was looking out to sea when he was presented with a grim sight: a lone, drifting corpse, a last chilling reminder

Above: 'Plane after plane after plane in formation one after the other ... and then "boom boom boom!"' – Ronald Jesse.
A Handley Page Halifax of No. 4 Group over the suburbs of Caen during Operation 'Charnwood'. 467 aircraft took part in the attack, which was originally intended to have bombed German strongpoints north of Caen, but the bombing area was shifted nearer the city because Allied troops were too close to the original targets. The raid devastated the northern suburbs.

of the ferocity of the fighting at sea off Normandy, perhaps even one of those lost in *Dragon*, or one of those sent to sink her: 'Last night during the first watch a dead-white corpse floated by on its back as though doing back stroke, as its limbs moved with gentle undulation. Floated past all the ships but no-one that we could see endeavoured to pick it up so that it could be identified and given decent burial.'

Captain Plawski of *Dragon* had visited *Belfast* the night before he lost his ship. Her loss turned out to be the last act in the Normandy campaign as far as *Belfast* was concerned. She weighed anchor and departed the gunline for the last time just after midday on 8 July, escorted by two motor launches and blasting one last shoot at a pair of German artillery batteries as she went. She was bound for home and a much needed refit. In total she spent 33 days in support of the landings, expending over 4,000 6-inch and 1,000 4-inch shells. By 18:00 she was once again anchored off Spithead.

As *Belfast* left the gunline, a signal arrived from the Commodore, Naval Force J (now in the Brook Smith Collection, IWM Department of Documents). It turned out to be a few lines of rhyme composed especially for the occasion. A fitting epitaph to her Normandy adventure, it began:

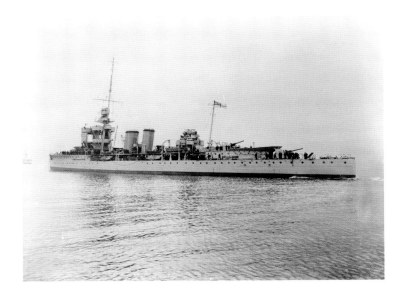

Above: 'Wretched *Dragon* hit by mine or torpedo ... for what use that old thing is she might just as well have not been here.'
– Peter Brooke Smith.
The Polish cruiser ORP *Dragon* in her heyday, when as HMS *Dragon* she had been the fastest ship in the fleet. She had the dubious honour of being one of only five warships destroyed by a human torpedo; the others were three minesweepers and the British destroyer *Quorn*.

Since first approach to Norman shore,
To crack the western wall,
Belfast has done good work and more,
With every cannon ball.
High out of range the Huns have run,
The fellows cannot take it,
Because of what your guns have done,
Our soldiers now can make it.

EPILOGUE

Of course, *Belfast*'s departure did not mark the end of the Battle for Normandy. It required two more brutal and costly offensives by Montgomery's 21st Army Group – Operation 'Atlantic' and Operation 'Goodwood' – before the rest of the battered city of Caen fell on 21 July. Four days later, the Americans broke out to the south of the beachhead in Operation 'Cobra', and on 15 August the Allies launched a second landing in the south of France – Operation 'Dragoon'. The German flank was now open, but Hitler condemned his armies to almost certain destruction by taking personal control, refusing to allow his commanders to withdraw, and even ordering a disastrous counter-attack. As a result, 50,000 troops were encircled in the Falaise Pocket when the Allied armies met on 21 August. Four days later, US and Free French troops liberated Paris. On 30 August, the German Army retreated across the River Seine, and Operation 'Overlord' was declared at an end. Eisenhower took direct control of all Allied ground forces on 1 September.

By this time, *Belfast* had left Normandy long behind. After stops at Portsmouth and Devonport, she returned to Scapa Flow on 12 July, where she went into dockyard hands for a long, tropical refit prior to joining the British Pacific Fleet. Many of her ship's company left for other ships, including Captain Frederick Parham ('left the ship very sadly'), who handed over command to Captain Royer M Dick on 29 July and went to stand by the brand new battleship HMS *Vanguard*, then building on the Clyde. It is, perhaps, a measure of the high esteem in which he was held that he was given command of the Royal Navy's last, and most powerful, battleship.

Belfast arrived in the Far East too late to take part in the final battles of the Pacific War. Her first mission was one of humanitarian relief work, evacuating former internees of the Japanese from Shanghai. She stayed in the Far East until October 1947 as flagship of the 5th Cruiser Squadron. After finally visiting the city whose name she bore for the first time since her launch in 1938, she returned to the Far East, playing a peripheral role in the Yangtse River incident in April 1949, when the sloop HMS *Amethyst* staged a dramatic escape down the river, under heavy fire from Communist Chinese artillery. *Belfast* refitted at Singapore, rejoining the fleet just in time to take part in the Korean War (1950–53), playing much the same role as she had off the coast of Normandy by providing heavy gunfire support to troops ashore. It was during this period that she was respectfully nicknamed 'that straight-shooting ship' by a US Navy admiral.

After the Korean War she returned to the UK and was placed in reserve, before being selected to undergo an extended refit and modernisation programme which took more than three years. She rejoined the fleet again in May 1959, and remained in service until 1963, before going into reserve, suffering the ignominy of becoming a floating barracks, and even losing her name, officially becoming the 'living ship' of the Reserve Ships Division at Portsmouth, HMS *Bellerophon*. She was saved from the scrap heap by a vigorous campaign led by one of her former commanding officers, Rear-Admiral Morgan Morgan-Giles, and was opened to the public on the River Thames near Tower Bridge on Trafalgar Day, 21 October 1971. In 1978, she became a branch of IWM.

As for her crew, nearly all of them left the Royal Navy after the war and resumed their interrupted civilian lives. Some, like Len Beardsley, were matter of fact about the ship: 'We paid off and that was it ... she'd not had a refit for some time I gather. So off we all went ... to me it was just a ship. I was leaving a ship and going off somewhere else to join another ship.'

Brian Butler remained involved in the Battle for Normandy, experiencing a very different aspect of this incredibly complex, multi-faceted operation:

> I was sent to Fort Southwick, which is on the Downs overlooking Portsmouth and that was the headquarters of the Allied Expeditionary Force. You could see nothing, it was just an old Victorian fort on the outside but when you got there, there was a mass of ... modern steel lined tunnels underground there with offices galore, with Wrens on teleprinters and people dashing around and the whole of the invasion was being run from there! I was only a young Able Seaman and ... I had a trolley. I had to push it round these offices and empty all the waste paper baskets out, and then when I'd done that I went down through a tunnel and opened a big pair of armoured doors which took me out on the Downs at the back of the fort ... I had a big incinerator there and I used to have to burn all the signals ... that were disposed of. That was a nice [job] but it didn't last very long, about three months and I was away to sea again ... it was a responsible job ... you had to be very careful, many a time I was chasing paper round the Downs!

Butler was phlegmatic about his time on the gunline:

The atmosphere was ok, we all just got on and did our job. There was no great excitement or anything like that ... once they got beyond the range of our guns then we just came back to Britain and I think once it finished we went up ... and we paid off and I left the *Belfast* ... it would have been August 1944.

Bernard Thomson was equally matter-of-fact about his role in what was arguably the most important military operation of the twentieth century: 'It was a bit lonely and frightening at times maybe', he recalled, 'but we just got on with it and the time seemed to go by rather fast ... there wasn't much to do other than mess about with your shells down there.' Denis Watkinson was reflective about the sacrifice, and with the benefit of hindsight, very aware of the risk involved:

I think it was so touch and go they kept a lot away from you, didn't want to put fear into everybody ... you can understand what would have happened if they'd planted fear into all them lads ... They would never have been able to get another landing if they'd lost that one ... I was only just 18 and what you're thinking is 'kill as many Germans as you can and get in and get the war over'. And don't forget we'd suffered bombing ... but when you look back and think of all those kids.

The final word, perhaps, should go to Bob Shrimpton who, although no less modest about his role, admirably sums up the thoughts of many veterans when they looked back on D-Day decades later: 'It was the most historical thing', he said simply, 'and I'm very proud to have been part of it. Very proud indeed.'

Right: Troops from 6th Battalion, The Green Howards, 69th Brigade, 50th (Northumbrian) Division, embarking onto the Infantry Landing Ship (LSI) *Empire Lance* at Southampton, 29 May 1944. Two battalions of Green Howards landed on Gold beach, under the guns of HMS *Belfast*. 7th Green Howards captured HMS *Belfast*'s first target, the German battery at La Marefontaine, on 6 June. Company Sergeant Major Stan Hollis of 6th Green Howards was awarded the only Victoria Cross of D-Day.

APPENDIX

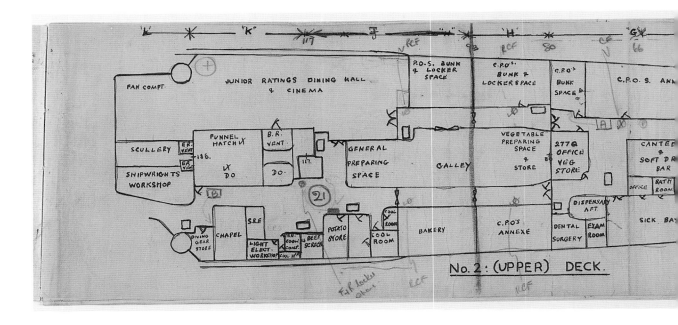

No. 2 : (UPPER) DECK.

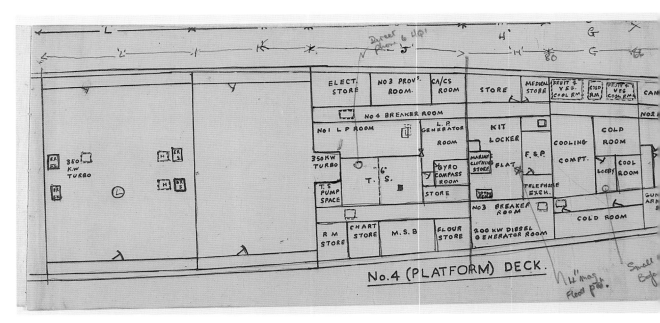

No. 4 (PLATFORM) DECK.

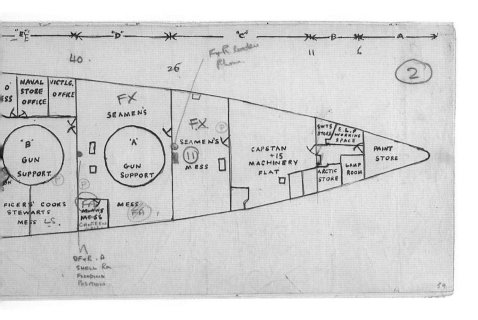

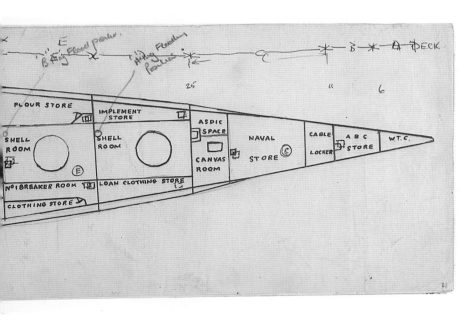

Plans of HMS *Belfast* taken from the Captain's Ship's Book, the official record of all tests and surveys. This volume covered the ship's post-war life from 1945 until 1965, two years after she had been placed in reserve. The bewildering and complex world that the *Belfast* men inhabited comprised nine decks and miles of compartments and passageways, from B Turret Shell Room deep down on the platform deck where Ron Jesse spent D-Day, up to the upper decks where Captain Parham observed 'one of the greatest, most important days in the whole history of the Empire'.

APPENDIX

Southampton Class Cruisers

Displacement:	9,100 tons
Length:	558 feet
Beam:	61¾ feet
Armament:	4 x triple 6-inch turret / 6 x twin 4-inch
Propulsion:	4 x Parsons Geared Turbines
Speed:	32 Knots
Group 1 (9,100 tons):	*Southampton, Newcastle, Birmingham, Glasgow, Sheffield*
Group 2 (9,400 tons):	*Liverpool, Manchester, Gloucester*
Group 3 (Improved *Southampton*, 10,000 tons):	
	Belfast, Edinburgh (*Belfast* later increased to 11,500 tons after reconstruction following mine damage in 1939)

Known D-Day Survivors

USS *Texas* (battleship). Museum ship at La Porte, Texas, USA.

HMS *Belfast* (cruiser). Museum ship in London, UK.

USS *Laffey* (destroyer). Museum ship at Charleston, South Carolina, USA.

ORP *Blyskawica* (destroyer). Museum ship in Gdynia, Poland.

HMS *Whimbrel* (sloop). In reserve in Egypt as ENS *Tariq*.

USS *Jeremiah O'Brien* (liberty ship). Museum ship at San Francisco, California.

LST 230 (landing ship, tank). Operational as Philippine Navy Ship *Laguna*.

LST 325 (landing ship, tank). Museum ship at Evansville, Indiana, USA.

LST 393 (landing ship, tank). Museum ship at Muskegon, Michigan, USA.

LST 510 (landing ship, tank). Operational as ferry, Long Island, New York, USA.

LCT 7074 (landing craft, tank). Undergoing restoration in Portsmouth, UK.

MGB 81 (motor gunboat). Restored and operating in Portsmouth, UK.

MTB 102 (motor torpedo boat). Restored and operating in Lowestoft, UK.

HDML 1387 (*Medusa*) (harbour defence motor launch). Restored and operating in Portsmouth, UK.

HDML 1309 (Morning Wings) (harbour defence motor launch). Privately owned in UK.

HSL 2561 (RAF air sea rescue launch). Houseboat at Hayling Island, UK.

Calshot (tender). Under restoration in Southampton, UK.

Challenge (tug). Under restoration at Shoreham, UK.

Devon Belle (tender; requisitioned launch). Based at Reading, UK.

Gralian (patrol vessel; requisitioned launch). Privately owned in UK.

*Hyperion (*War Department launch). Privately owned in UK.

Ryde (anti-aircraft ship; requisitioned passenger ferry). Derelict in Ryde, Isle of Wight, UK.

Bombardment Force E

Belfast (flagship):	Royal Navy (RN) 6-inch gun cruiser
Diadem:	RN 5.25-inch gun anti-aircraft cruiser

Kempenfelt:	RN 'W'-class destroyer
Faulknor:	RN 'F'-class destroyer
Fury:	RN 'F'-class destroyer
Venus:	RN 'V'-class destroyer
Vigilant:	RN 'V'-class destroyer
Algonquin:	Royal Canadian Navy (RCN) 'Tribal'-class destroyer
Sioux:	RCN 'Tribal'-class destroyer
Bleasdale:	RN 'Hunt'-class escort destroyer
Stevenstone:	RN 'Hunt'-class escort destroyer
Glaisdale:	Royal Norwegian Navy 'Hunt'-class escort destroyer
La Combattante:	Free French 'Hunt'-class escort destroyer

Close Support Craft
7 landing craft (gun; 2 x 4.7in)
8 LCT (rocket; 792 5in R/P)
6 landing craft support (light; 1 x 2 pdr)
6 landing craft (Flak; 4 x 2 pdr, 8 x 20mm AA)
plus 4 embarked SP artillery regiments

SOURCES

PRIMARY SOURCES
The National Archives
Log 1: Log of HMS *Belfast* at TNA ADM 53/118968
Log 2: Log of HMS *Belfast* at TNA ADM 53/118969

IWM Department of Documents
IWM Documents. 20637 Brooke Smith, Lieutenant W Peter
IWM Documents. 22906 Bunbury, Charles
IWM Documents. 2823 Gower, Captain J R
IWM Documents. 1755 Jones, A

IWM Sound Archive
To locate the source of an interview quoted in this book, search the following list
by surname:

IWM Sound 26948 Beardsley, Len
IWM Sound 26953 Bonner, Alec
IWM Sound 29022 Brown, Robert 'Bert'
IWM Sound 24905 Burnett, Arthur
IWM Sound 25217 Burridge, George
IWM Sound 25052 Butler, Brian
IWM Sound 27228 Coleman, Leslie

IWM Sound 26746 Fursland, Arthur 'Larry'
IWM Sound 25186 Jesse, Ronald
IWM Sound 25240 Jones, David
IWM Sound 26747 Painter, Gordon 'Putty'
IWM Sound 27742 Palmer, Edward 'Andy'
IWM Sound 14128 Parham, Frederick
IWM Sound 21735 Shrimpton, Bob 'Ping'
IWM Sound 24907 Simpson, Charles
IWM Sound 6203 Stagno, Joseph
IWM Sound 27746 Stanley, George
IWM Sound 27489 Thomson, Bernard
IWM Sound 28765 Tyler, Lance
IWM Sound 27461 Watkinson, Denis

PUBLISHED WORKS

Stephen E Ambrose, *D-Day. June 6, 1944: The Battle for the Normandy Beaches* (Simon and Schuster, London, 2002)

Roderick Bailey, *Forgotten Voices of D-Day* (Ebury Press in association with the Imperial War Museum, 2010)

I C B Dear and M R D Foot, *The Oxford Companion to World War II* (Oxford University Press, 2001)

Commander William Donald, DSC and Bar, *Stand By For Action* (New English Library, 1975)

Remy Desquenes, *Memorial Caen Normandie No. 4: 6th June 1944 Gold Beach Asnelles* (Editions Oeust-France, Normandie, 1990)

Jonathan Falconer, *D-Day Operations Manual* (Haynes Publishing, Sparkford, Somerset, 2013)

Sir David Fraser, *Alanbrooke* (London, 1982)

Max Hastings, *Overlord: D-Day and the Battle for Normandy 1944* (Book Club Associates, 1984)

Nick Hewitt, 'Landing Craft', *Military History Monthly*, issue 47, 2014

Nick Hewitt, 'HMS *Belfast* and Operation 'Neptune' June–July 1944', *The Mariners' Mirror*, vol. 94, issue 2, May 2008

David Lee, *Beachhead Assault: The Story of the Royal Naval Commandos in World War II* (Greenhill Books, London, 2006)

Paul Lund and Harry Ludlum, *The War of the Landing Craft* (New English Library, London, 1976)

Michael Reynolds, *Steel Inferno: 1 SS Panzer Corps in Normandy* (Spellmount, Staplehurst, 1997)

Captain S W Roskill, DSC, RN, *The War At Sea: Volume III The Offensive Part II* (HMSO, London, 1961)

John Wingate, DSC, *In Trust for the Nation: HMS Belfast 1939–1972* (revised edition, Imperial War Museum, London, 2004)

David Woodward, *Ramsey at War: The Fighting Life of Admiral Sir Bertram Ramsey, KCB, KBE, MVO* (William Kimber, London, 1957)

ONLINE

CWGC (Commonwealth War Graves Commission): www.cwgc.org
www.oisterwijk- marketgarden.com/la_marefontaine_battery.html
Naval History.net: www.naval-history.net/

CREDITS

All images © IWM unless otherwise stated. Every effort has been made to contact all copyright holders, the publishers will be glad to make good in future editions any error or omissions brought to their attention.

8 (A 20686), 10 (IWM ART 16801), 11 (HU 16012), 12 top (HU 46128) © Artist's Estate, 12 bottom (IWM Sound 24907), 13 top (IWM Sound 28765), 13 centre (IWM Sound 24905) © Photographer's Estate, 13 bottom (A 20687), 14 top (IWM Sound 27746) 14 centre (IWM Sound 25240), 14 bottom (IWM Sound 26746), 15 top (IWM Sound 25217), 15 bottom (IWM Sound 26953), 18 (IWM ART LD 4459), 19 top (IWM Sound 25052), 19 bottom (IWM Sound 25186), 20 (IWM Sound 21735), 22 (A 23094), 24 (A 23671), 27 left (A 23992), 27 right (EA 64465), 29 (MH 24822), 30 (TR 1631), 31 (A 23932), 32 (D 18163), 33 (A 23720a), 35 left (A 27906), 35 right (A 16176), 36 top (A 23752), 36 bottom (A 24018), 37 (A 24484), 38 (MH 3660), 39 (H 39300), 40 (H 39297), 42 (A 25665), 43 (IWM Sound 27228), 44 (IWM Sound 26948), 46 (NYT 27247), 48 (A 18666), 51 (HU 65372) © Richard Tosswill, 55 (A 23731), 56 (EA 25357), 57 (IWM ART LD 4774), 58 (A 24184), 63 (A 23718a), 64 (IWM ART LD 4390), 66 (B 5098), 67 (IWM ART LD 4587), 68 (A 23937), 70 (MH 24804), 71 left (IWM FLM 4021), 71 right (IWM FLM 4015), 72 (IWM Sound 26747), 74 (IWM Sound 27461), 75 (IWM ART LD 4372), 76 (A 24101), 77 (A 29320), 78 (IWM ART LD 4277), 79 (B 5225), 80 (A 23935), 81 (B 5014), 83 (IWM FLM 2568), 84 (MGH 3381) Courtesy of George Stevens, Jr., 85 (A 24342), 86 top (IWM Sound 29022), 86 bottom (IWM Sound 27489), 87 (A 24343), 88 ((MGH 3381) Courtesy of George Stevens, Jr., 89 (B 5259), 91 (A 23933), 92 (CL 40), 93 (C 4841), 94 (IWM ART LD 4761), 95 top (B 5689), 95 bottom (A 24084), 96 (A 24675), 97 (A 24104), 99 (IWM ART LD 4280), 100 (BU 1190), 101 (MGH 3381) Courtesy of George Stevens, Jr., 102 (IWM ART 16569) Permission of Mrs Susan Russell Flint, 103 (A 23925), 104 (B 5128), 109 (IWM ART 4381), 111 (A 23994), 112 (B 5135), 114 (CL 631), 117 (A 24364), 119 (IWM ART LD 4504), 120 (A 24427), 121 (B 8032), 123 (A 24725), 126 (B 5354), 127 (B 5359), 128 (C 4663), 130 top (IWM ART 4366), 130 bottom (A 24324), 131 (A 24674), 132 (A 24004), 135 (B 6060), 136 (MH 24897), 137 top (IWM ART LD 5445), 137 bottom (A 24628), 138 (EA 26319), 139 (EA 25734), 141 (A 24092), 142 top (A 24327), 142 bottom (A 23946), 143 (B 5859), 144 (B 7218), 145 (IWM ART LD 4392), 146 left (IWM ART LD 4598), 146 right (IWM ART LD 4456), 147 (IWM ART LD 4461), 148 (FL 7061), 151 (IWM ART LD 4712), 152 (IWM ART LD 5816), 154 (IWM ART LD 5560), 158 (MH 1402), 159 (B 6642), 160 left (IWM ART LD 4367), 160 right (IWM ART LD 4389), 162 (CL 347), 163 (SP 2503), 167 (B 5237), 168–169 (Documents.13300)

ART

p.10, *HMS Belfast on Northern Patrol captures the German blockade runner 'Cap Norte' 13,615 tons 9th October 1939* by Harold Wyllie

p.19, *In a 6 Inch Gun-turret* by Stephen Bone

p.57, *LCT and LSM on their Way to Normandy* by Stephen Bone

p.64, *At Sea on an LCI (Landing Craft, Infantry)* by Edward Ardizzone

p.67, *Preparations for D-Day* by Robert Eurich

p.75, *First Sight of Normandy* by Stephen Bone

p.78, *From the Landing Craft Assault: we watched the 'planes dive-bombing near Le Hamel, D Day, 6th June 1944* by J C Heath

p.94, *High Tide in the Gooseberry Harbour* by Stephen Bone

p.99, *We Lie at the Beach Dressing Station and Wonder how the Battle is Going : D Day 6th June 1944* by J C Heath

p.102, *HMS Belfast, Normandy, 8 July 1944* by Frank Russell Flint

p.109, *Off the Normandy Beaches* by Stephen Bone

INDEX